MAKE

MONEY

FROM

MONEY

By

Lalit Mohanty

Please Review this Book

PREFACE

In a world where financial stability is often tied to the hours we work, there exists a group of people who play by a different set of rules. These individuals have discovered that true wealth is not achieved through hard work alone, but rather through the art of making money work for them. This book, *Make Money from Money*, is written to inspire a fundamental shift in how you think about money, work, and wealth.

As someone who has navigated the journey from working for a paycheck to building passive income streams, I've experienced firsthand the transformation that comes from harnessing money's potential. While society encourages us to study hard, get good jobs, and secure stable incomes, it often overlooks the essential knowledge of wealth creation—knowledge that allows one to build assets and gain financial independence. The wealthy don't simply work for money; they create systems and structures that enable them to earn even while they sleep. They master money rather than letting it dictate their lives, seeing it not as a reward to spend but as a tool to multiply.

In this book, we'll dive into the concepts that empower people to generate lasting wealth, going beyond the paycheck and the typical financial limitations many of us know. We'll explore how to identify and build assets that generate income, the crucial difference between assets and liabilities, and why a job is often a short-term solution to a long-term problem. You'll read real-world examples that illustrate the journey from worker to wealth creator, such as my experience building passive income by renting out cabins, which surpassed the income of a friend working tirelessly in a traditional job. Through stories like this, I hope to illuminate the potential that lies in seeing money not as an end goal, but as the starting point for greater financial opportunities.

This book will also introduce the power of structures like corporations, which enable wealth growth and reduce tax burdens, and we'll examine the capitalist system's role in providing pathways to financial freedom. Along the way, you'll find practical advice on shifting your mindset to one that values long-term wealth over short-term gains, transforming your financial habits, and embracing the discipline and patience required to succeed.

Whether you're just beginning to think about financial independence or are already on the path, *Make Money from Money* aims to be a guide that helps you make informed choices about building wealth. My hope is that this book inspires you to take control of your financial future and start creating systems that allow your money to work for you. As you read through these chapters, may you discover the strategies, mindset, and motivation needed to transform your financial life and achieve the freedom you've always desired.

Lalit Prasad Mohanty

ADVANCE
BOLLINGER
BANDS

With Ai Codes for Algo Trading

by
Lalit Mohanty

Escaping the
MIDDLE
CLASS
TRAP

Through Smart Investing

by
Lalit Mohanty

Advanced
TRADING
PSYCHOLOGY

With Practical Examples

by
Lalit Mohanty

ADVANCE
RISK
MANAGEMENT
IN
TRADING

by
Lalit Mohanty

Table of Contents

- **Building a Portfolio of Assets:** Examples of assets that can be created or acquired to generate income, and how these assets provide financial independence over time.

- **Asset vs. Liability Mindset:** How adopting this mindset is crucial for long-term wealth-building.

Chapter 3: Money: A Bad Master but a Good Slave

- **Mastering Money, Not the Other Way Around:** Money should serve you, not control you. When money is viewed as a means to acquire assets rather than just as income to spend, it becomes a powerful tool.

- **Psychological Shift:** Wealthy people view money as an instrument to create more wealth rather than a reward to spend immediately. This chapter discusses the discipline and patience needed to use money effectively.

Chapter 4: The Art of Capitalism and Making Money from Money

- **Capitalism's Role in Wealth Creation:** Capitalism enables individuals to create and invest in assets that can grow in value and produce returns.

- **Money-Making Mechanisms:** From real estate and stocks to entrepreneurial ventures, the wealthy invest in opportunities that allow their money to multiply.

- **Real-Life Example:** The example of your friend working as a private school tutor versus renting wood cabins is explored in detail, showcasing how owning assets can be a more effective strategy for wealth accumulation than trading time for money.

Chapter 5: Why a Job is a Short-Term Solution to a Long-Term Problem

- **Limitations of Salaries:** Jobs offer stability but are limited in wealth-building potential. The job itself is a form of active income, where earnings are capped and directly tied to hours worked.

- **The Financial Trap of a Job:** Working solely for a paycheck often restricts people from experiencing the financial freedom they desire.

- **Importance of Creating Money:** Creating passive income through assets provides financial security and independence, freeing individuals from the constraints of salary-based income.

Chapter 6: Making Money by Investing Capital: Case Study of the Wood Cabins

- **Real-World Application of Asset Creation:**

  - *The Setup:* Your friend earns a steady salary as a tutor, working for hours to earn an income.

  - *Your Investment:* By renting wood cabins and sub-leasing them at a higher rate, you've generated passive income with minimal effort. This example illustrates how capital, when strategically invested, can yield higher returns with less work.

- o **Lesson:** Smart investments can outperform salaried jobs over time. Leveraging resources like real estate for rental income demonstrates the potential of passive income streams.

Chapter 7: The Power of Corporations in Wealth Creation and Tax Savings

- **Corporations as Tools for Financial Growth:** Wealthy individuals often establish corporations to structure their financial activities, benefiting from various tax-saving advantages.

- **Saving on Taxes Through Corporations:** Corporations provide opportunities to deduct expenses, reinvest profits, and legally minimize tax obligations, helping individuals retain more of their earnings.

- **How Corporations Reduce Liability:** Corporations shield personal wealth and allow for growth with minimized risk, making them an essential part of a wealth-building strategy.

Chapter 8: The Psychology of Wealth: Developing a Wealth-Building Mindset

- **Adopting a Wealthy Mindset:** Shifting from consumer thinking to investor thinking is crucial. Wealthy people view each dollar as an employee working for them.

- **Discipline and Patience:** Long-term wealth requires a mindset of delayed gratification, allowing assets to grow and produce income over time.

- **Continuous Learning and Growth:** The most successful individuals remain students of finance, always learning new strategies and staying open to emerging wealth-creating opportunities.

Chapter 9: Practical Steps to Begin Making Money from Money

- **Identify and Assess Opportunities:** Evaluate potential investments in real estate, stocks, and other assets.

- **Start Small, Think Big:** Begin by allocating a portion of your income to building or acquiring assets, with the goal of expanding as passive income increases.

- **Utilize Your Capital Wisely:** Invest wisely with a focus on long-term gains rather than quick returns. Learn to see each dollar as an investment in your future wealth.

Chapter 10: Conclusion: Embracing Financial Freedom

- **Becoming a Money Maker, Not a Money Earner:** The journey to financial freedom requires understanding money's potential as a tool for creating more wealth.

- **Building a Legacy:** True wealth is created over time and serves as a legacy, continuing to generate income and create opportunities for future generations.

- **Living on Your Terms:** The ultimate goal of wealth-building is financial independence, allowing you to live life on your own terms, supported by the assets you've built.

CHAPTER 1

WHY THE RICH DON'T WORK FOR MONEY; THEY CREATE MONEY

The Concept of the Rat Race

In our society, most people spend the majority of their lives chasing money, constantly working harder, climbing the corporate ladder, and living paycheck to paycheck. This cycle is often referred to as the "rat race"—a relentless pursuit that keeps people perpetually busy but ultimately unfulfilled. In the rat race, people are tied to a routine of working to pay bills, with little or no time to think about or invest in their long-term financial security. But the wealthy operate differently; they don't work for money in the traditional sense. Instead, they focus on creating systems and investing in assets that allow them to make money without direct involvement.

The rat race traps people by convincing them that the only way to achieve financial stability is through a steady job. It teaches that the more one works, the more secure they'll become. But in reality, relying solely on a job to build wealth rarely leads to financial freedom. Salaries, while providing a predictable income, are limited by hours, energy, and the market's willingness to pay. Many people work hard and earn more over time, but their expenses often increase along with their income, keeping them in the same financial cycle. The wealthy, on the other hand, break free from this cycle by understanding that time is their most valuable resource—and they choose to spend it creating wealth-generating opportunities.

The Difference Between Working for Money and Creating Money

For most people, the primary way to earn money is through active income, where time and effort are directly exchanged for money. Active income is derived from a job or any work that pays a salary, hourly wage, or fee for services. While active income provides stability, it's finite—limited by how much one can work. Once you stop working, the income stops.

The wealthy, however, see money as a resource that can be leveraged to generate passive income, a form of income that continues to flow in even without direct effort. This is the essence of creating money, not just earning it. The rich view money as a tool they can invest in income-generating assets like real estate, stocks, or businesses. These assets have the potential to grow in value and produce ongoing income, freeing the wealthy from the need to work constantly for money.

Instead of focusing on how much they can make by working, they focus on how much they can make by building assets. By creating or acquiring assets, the wealthy build systems that generate money on their behalf, allowing them to escape the time-for-money exchange that defines the rat race.

Why Working for Money Alone Doesn't Lead to Wealth

To understand why the rich don't focus solely on working for money, it's helpful to consider the limitations of relying on a salary:

1. **Limited by Time:** There are only so many hours in a day. No matter how much a person earns per hour, they are limited by the time they can physically work.

2. **No Freedom:** When income is tied directly to hours worked, financial security becomes dependent on maintaining that job or profession. This leads to a lack of freedom, as any interruption in work means an interruption in income.

3. **Tax Burden:** Salaried employees often pay higher taxes than those who generate income from investments. When income is generated through passive sources like investments, there are often more tax-efficient ways to grow wealth, reducing the burden and increasing overall net income.

4. **Inflation and Cost of Living:** Salary increases often lag behind inflation and rising living costs, which means that even though a person's salary might increase over time, it's not enough to keep up with the increased cost of goods, housing, and other necessities. This makes it difficult for salaried workers to accumulate real wealth.

5. **Lifestyle Inflation:** As people earn more, they tend to spend more, leading to lifestyle inflation. Their spending often rises with their earnings, leaving them no better off in terms of financial security or freedom.

By contrast, when people focus on creating money through assets, they're not tied to these limitations. They are able to accumulate wealth that grows independently of their daily efforts, allowing them to enjoy more financial stability and freedom over time.

How the Rich Create Money

The rich achieve financial freedom by prioritizing assets over salaries. Here are some key ways they do it:

1. **Investing in Real Estate:** One of the most popular ways the wealthy create money is by investing in real estate. When someone owns rental properties, for example, the property generates monthly income without the owner needing to work for it. The value of real estate tends to appreciate over time, allowing for both income and capital growth.

2. **Building Businesses:** Many wealthy individuals own or invest in businesses. By creating a business, they generate an income stream that can grow over time, sometimes reaching a point where they can step back from daily operations while still profiting from its success.

3. **Stocks and Dividends:** The wealthy often invest in stocks, which allows them to earn through dividends or capital gains. Dividend-paying stocks provide regular income, while growth stocks offer the potential for appreciation in value over time.

4. **Royalties and Licensing:** Some wealthy people create intellectual property—such as books, music, patents, or online courses—that can generate royalties or licensing income. This type of income continues long after the initial work is done, creating passive income streams.

5. **Private Equity and Venture Capital:** Wealthy individuals often participate in private equity or venture capital investments, where they invest in promising startups or private businesses. If the business succeeds, they can see significant returns, creating substantial wealth without ongoing work.

The Mindset Shift: From Earning to Creating Money

To escape the rat race, it's essential to adopt a mindset shift from earning money to creating money. This requires understanding that wealth is built by owning or creating assets that generate ongoing income, rather than relying on a job for security. It's about seeing each dollar as an employee that can be put to work, generating more income.

This shift in mindset is a major reason the wealthy continue to grow their wealth while others struggle to get ahead. They understand that real financial freedom comes from building streams of income that flow regardless of daily efforts. When they have assets that generate passive income, they're able to spend their time and energy on activities that bring them joy or align with their values, without worrying about how they'll pay their bills.

Breaking Free from the Rat Race

Escaping the rat race doesn't mean quitting a job tomorrow or giving up a career. Instead, it involves a gradual process of building assets and shifting priorities. Here are steps you can take to begin:

1. **Identify Your Financial Goals:** Start by defining what financial freedom means to you. What kind of income would allow you to step back from your job? How much would you need to live comfortably without actively working?

2. **Create an Investment Plan:** Consider ways to gradually invest in assets. This could mean setting aside a portion of your income to invest in stocks, real estate, or other income-generating opportunities.

3. **Reduce Liabilities and Build Capital:** Avoid lifestyle inflation and use your income to save and invest. This will allow you to acquire assets rather than accumulating debt or unnecessary expenses.

4. **Think Long Term:** Wealth creation takes time. Focus on long-term gains rather than immediate returns, and develop the patience needed to let your investments grow.

5. **Continue Learning:** Financial freedom requires ongoing education and awareness of new opportunities. Study investment strategies, personal finance, and wealth-building techniques, and apply this knowledge to your financial journey.

Understanding Wealth-Building: Wealth is Created Through Ownership and Investments, Not Just Earning a Salary

Introduction to Wealth-Building

For many people, wealth-building seems like a distant goal, one that requires either luck or a high-paying job to achieve.

But if we look closely at how wealthy individuals actually create their wealth, it becomes clear that their path is not just about earning a high salary or saving diligently. The key lies in building wealth through ownership and investments, leveraging resources to create financial security and independence.

Moving Beyond Salary: Why Earnings Alone Aren't Enough

The traditional financial path—go to school, get a good job, and work hard to earn a salary—has limitations when it comes to building significant wealth. A salary, no matter how high, is an active form of income. It requires a person to trade their time and effort for money, creating a dependency on work for financial security.

Here's why relying solely on a salary limits wealth-building:

1. **Finite Time:** There are only so many hours in a day, which means that income is capped by the amount of time a person can realistically work.

2. **Direct Dependency on Employment:** Relying solely on a job creates a dependency on external factors, like the employer's stability or the economic climate, which can impact income security.

3. **Inflation Erodes Value:** Over time, the purchasing power of a salary can decline if wages don't keep pace with inflation. Relying on a salary alone makes it harder to keep up with rising costs, let alone get ahead financially.

Wealthy individuals understand these limitations. They focus on making money through assets, which grow in value or generate income independently of their direct involvement, creating a form of financial security that doesn't rely on continuous work.

The Power of Ownership: Building Assets for Wealth

Ownership of income-generating assets is one of the primary ways the wealthy build and sustain wealth. Assets are resources or investments that have intrinsic value and the potential to increase in worth over time, generate income, or both. Assets work on the owner's behalf, often with little or no direct involvement, allowing wealth to grow passively.

Here are some common types of assets that create wealth through ownership:

1. **Real Estate:** One of the most popular and effective assets for building wealth is real estate. Properties such as residential rentals, commercial spaces, or land can generate rental income and often appreciate in value over time. A single property might yield a monthly income stream while also growing in worth, creating dual benefits for the owner. Real estate also provides the opportunity to leverage funds through mortgages, allowing the owner to control more valuable properties with relatively small initial investments.

2. **Stocks and Equities:** When someone invests in stocks, they own a portion of a company. Stocks can appreciate in value, offering the chance to sell at a profit, while many stocks also pay dividends, providing a regular income stream. Over time, the stock market tends to grow in value, creating wealth for investors who hold diversified, long-term portfolios.

3. **Businesses:** Owning a business can be one of the most powerful ways to build wealth. When someone owns a profitable business, they benefit from the income it generates and any appreciation in the business's value. Business ownership provides both active income (if the owner is involved) and passive income (if the owner hires others to manage it). Many wealthy individuals invest in or start businesses with the goal of generating ongoing revenue without their constant involvement.

4. **Intellectual Property and Royalties:** Intellectual property, such as patents, books, music, or software, can provide long-lasting income through royalties or licensing. For example, an author might earn royalties on a book for years after it's published, or a software developer could license a tool to companies worldwide. Intellectual property requires initial effort but can yield ongoing income streams without continuous work.

5. **Bonds and Interest-Bearing Investments:** Bonds and other interest-bearing investments provide predictable income over time. Although bonds may offer lower returns than other assets, they are generally less volatile and offer a reliable stream of income that can contribute to financial stability.

Wealth Creation Through Investments

Investments play a crucial role in wealth-building because they allow money to grow over time without requiring additional labor from the investor. Investments essentially enable money to "work" for the individual, producing returns that contribute to overall wealth. Wealthy individuals recognize that money invested today has the potential to multiply in the future, making it essential to allocate a portion of income toward investment opportunities.

Here's how investments contribute to wealth-building:

1. **Compounding Returns:** Compounding is one of the most powerful concepts in wealth-building. When returns on investments are reinvested, they generate earnings on previous earnings, causing the investment to grow at an accelerated rate over time. For instance, if someone invests in a stock with dividends and reinvests those dividends, they benefit from a compounding effect that builds wealth exponentially.

2. **Diversification of Income:** By investing in various asset classes (stocks, bonds, real estate), wealthy individuals create diversified income streams. This diversification protects them from market volatility, as losses in one area can be offset by gains in another, providing more stability and resilience to their wealth portfolio.

3. **Appreciation Over Time:** Most assets have the potential to increase in value over time, allowing investors to accumulate wealth through appreciation. Whether it's real estate, stocks, or a business, assets grow in value, contributing to an increase in overall net worth. Wealthy individuals invest in assets with appreciation potential, allowing them to passively grow wealth over the years.

4. **Tax Advantages:** Certain investments offer tax benefits that allow investors to retain more of their earnings. For instance, real estate investments often provide tax deductions for property-related expenses, and long-term capital gains are typically taxed at a

lower rate than ordinary income. This enables wealthy individuals to build wealth more efficiently by minimizing their tax liabilities.

Creating Financial Security Through Assets

Financial security is achieved not through a high salary but through income-generating assets that continue to produce even during times of economic uncertainty. Wealthy people understand that true security comes from having control over assets that generate consistent income, regardless of external factors. This concept is known as *financial resilience*—the ability to maintain income and stability even when job opportunities or economic conditions fluctuate.

Here's how assets contribute to financial security:

1. **Freedom from Employment Dependency:** When assets generate income, individuals don't have to rely solely on a job for financial stability. This freedom from employment dependency provides a sense of security and control over their financial future.

2. **Income Stability and Predictability:** Income from assets like real estate or dividends provides regular cash flow, making it easier to manage living expenses, save, and invest further. Even during economic downturns, asset income can offer a financial buffer, allowing individuals to withstand uncertainty with less stress.

3. **Generational Wealth:** Assets that generate income and appreciate over time create wealth that can be passed down to future generations. Many wealthy families focus on building assets not just for themselves but as a legacy for their children and

grandchildren, creating a source of long-term financial security for the family.

Shifting the Focus to Asset-Building

Most people have been conditioned to think in terms of earning a salary and spending it on living expenses, with little left over for building wealth. Wealthy individuals, however, prioritize allocating funds to assets first, focusing on building wealth before increasing their lifestyle expenses. This shift in focus from consumption to investment is one of the core differences between those who build wealth and those who remain in the rat race.

Here's how to begin shifting your focus to asset-building:

1. **Pay Yourself First:** Allocate a portion of each paycheck toward investments before spending on discretionary items. By paying yourself first, you make wealth-building a priority.

2. **Avoid Debt That Doesn't Generate Income:** Wealthy individuals distinguish between "good debt" (debt used to acquire income-generating assets) and "bad debt" (debt used for consumption). Avoid debt that doesn't contribute to income generation, like credit card debt for lifestyle expenses.

3. **Reinvest Returns:** Instead of spending investment returns, reinvest them to build your wealth further. Reinvesting creates a compounding effect that accelerates growth and enhances financial security.

4. **Live Below Your Means:** Living below your means frees up more capital for investment. Wealthy individuals often practice financial discipline by

spending less than they earn, enabling them to allocate more resources toward assets.

CHAPTER 2

UNDERSTANDING ASSETS AND LIABILITIES

In order to build wealth, one must first understand the fundamental financial principles that shape how money flows in and out of your life. This chapter explores two of the most crucial concepts in personal finance: **Assets** and **Liabilities**. Grasping the difference between these two will lay the foundation for making smart financial decisions and moving towards financial independence.

What is an Asset?

An **asset** is anything that puts money in your pocket. Assets are income-generating tools that help you grow your wealth over time. These are the things that work for you, contributing to your cash flow and providing financial security. When you have more assets than liabilities, you are on your way to achieving financial freedom.

Examples of assets include:

- **Rental Properties**: Real estate is one of the most common types of assets. Rental properties, whether residential or commercial, provide regular income in the form of rent payments. Over time, they can also appreciate in value, increasing your net worth. The key is that these properties bring in money (rent) without you needing to actively work for it.

- **Stocks and Dividends**: Stocks can provide returns through dividends and capital appreciation. When you buy shares in a company, you're essentially purchasing ownership. The company may pay you dividends—a portion of its profits—on a regular basis. Additionally, if the value of the stock increases, you can sell it for a profit.

- **Businesses**: Owning a business is one of the most effective ways to create wealth. A business can generate consistent income, especially if it's structured well and operated efficiently. With a successful business, the income continues even if you're not actively working in it.

- **Bonds**: Bonds are essentially loans you make to corporations or governments. In return, the bond issuer pays you periodic interest (coupon payments) until the bond matures. When a bond matures, you receive the principal amount back.

- **Royalties and Intellectual Property**: This category includes patents, trademarks, copyrights, and other intellectual property. If you own intellectual property, you can earn royalties every time it's used by others, whether it's a song, invention, book, or product design.

The key takeaway here is that assets are investments that generate positive cash flow or increase in value over time. They work for you, earning you money passively.

What is a Liability?

A **liability**, on the other hand, is anything that takes money out of your pocket. Liabilities are expenses or financial obligations that demand cash on a regular basis. These are the things that drain your resources and impede your financial progress. Unlike assets, liabilities do not generate income—they often require active work or spending to maintain.

Examples of liabilities include:

- **Loans**: Personal loans, student loans, credit card debt, and mortgages are all liabilities. While these loans may have a useful purpose (e.g., buying a home or financing education), they represent money that you owe and must pay back with interest. The more debt you carry, the more money you spend paying off the interest and principal.

- **Cars**: Most cars are liabilities, especially when they are financed through loans. While they provide utility, they depreciate over time and often require costly maintenance, insurance, and repairs. Additionally, if you have a car loan, the car becomes an asset only when it helps you generate income—such as if it's used for a rideshare business—but for most people, it's a drain on cash flow.

- **Luxury Items**: Things like designer clothing, jewelry, expensive watches, and collectibles can be liabilities. While they may hold personal value, they often do not generate income. Instead, they usually require a constant flow of money to maintain or store and depreciate in value over time.

- **Credit Card Balances**: If you carry balances on your credit cards, the interest charges quickly accumulate, making it harder to build wealth. Unlike a productive asset, the money used to pay down credit card debt does not provide a return.

- **Rental Property Liabilities**: If you own a rental property but have a mortgage on it, the mortgage is a liability. The property itself may generate income, but if expenses like maintenance, property management, and interest payments exceed the rental income, it becomes a drain on your finances.

Why Understanding the Difference Matters

The key to financial success is accumulating assets while minimizing liabilities. The more assets you have, the more money flows into your pocket. The more liabilities you have, the more money flows out. Here's how the two affect your financial journey:

- **Assets put money in your pocket**: As your assets grow, they provide a steady stream of income, increasing your cash flow without needing to work harder or longer hours. This is where the rich focus their attention—on building assets that work for them.

- **Liabilities take money out of your pocket**: Liabilities, particularly those that don't add value or appreciate over time, increase your financial burden. They may create short-term comfort but often delay long-term financial success. The wealthiest people understand that reducing liabilities is essential to increasing their wealth.

Building Wealth: Shift from Liabilities to Assets

If you are serious about financial freedom, you need to gradually shift your focus from liabilities to assets. This doesn't mean living a life of deprivation, but it does involve being strategic with your spending. Here are some steps to make the shift:

1. **Track your spending**: Start by understanding where your money is going. Are you spending on items that will depreciate or items that can help you earn money (like an investment in stocks, real estate, or education)?

2. **Invest in income-generating assets**: Rather than accumulating more liabilities (such as luxury items or cars), focus on acquiring things that generate passive income. This could mean investing in real estate, purchasing dividend stocks, or starting a business.

3. **Pay off high-interest debts**: If you have liabilities like credit card debt, make it a priority to pay them off. High-interest debts can prevent you from building wealth and keeping money flowing out of your pocket.

4. **Build an emergency fund**: Having an emergency fund is a safeguard against unexpected expenses that might otherwise force you into taking on more debt (i.e., liabilities). This provides peace of mind and financial stability.

5. **Leverage debt strategically**: Not all debt is bad. You can use debt as a tool to acquire assets—such as a mortgage for a rental property. The key is that the income from the asset (the rent) should exceed the cost of the debt (the mortgage payments).

The Role of Cash Flow

One of the key differences between assets and liabilities lies in their **cash flow impact. Cash flow** is the net amount of money coming in versus the money going out of your financial life.

- **Assets provide positive cash flow**: Rental properties provide monthly rent payments, stocks offer dividends, and businesses generate profits. These sources of income flow directly into your pocket, helping you fund your lifestyle without having to actively work for it.

- **Liabilities cause negative cash flow**: Liabilities, like loans or luxury items, create recurring payments that must be made, pulling money out of your pocket. For instance, a car loan requires monthly payments, and if that car doesn't generate any income (such as being used for a rideshare business), it's simply a liability.

The real secret to wealth-building is to make sure the **positive cash flow from assets exceeds the negative cash flow from liabilities**. This will put you on the path to financial independence, where your passive income from assets can support your lifestyle, freeing you from the need to work a traditional job.

The Power of Compounding Assets

While liabilities can drag you down with interest payments and ongoing costs, **assets—especially those that earn interest or dividends—can grow exponentially** over time due to the power of **compounding**.

- **Interest and Dividends**: For example, when you invest in stocks or bonds, the dividends or interest you earn can be reinvested, which increases the amount of capital you have working for you. Over time, this compounding effect can turn a modest initial investment into a sizable fortune. For instance, if you invest $1,000 at a 10% annual return, after a year you'd have $1,100. Reinvesting that $100 increase next year leads to even greater growth.

- **Real Estate Appreciation**: The value of well-chosen real estate typically appreciates over time, meaning the value of your asset increases. This can lead to **capital gains** when you sell, and even if you hold on to the property, its rising value can lead to higher rental income due to increased demand or market changes.

In contrast, liabilities don't benefit from compounding. A loan you owe doesn't magically reduce the interest burden—it grows the longer you carry it. The more liabilities you have, the more money you need to spend paying interest, leaving you with fewer resources to invest in assets.

Building Wealth through a Systematic Approach

While the basic concept of assets versus liabilities is simple, the real challenge is how to **systematically acquire assets** while **minimizing liabilities**. Here's how you can approach this:

1. **Start with Cash Flow Assets**: Begin by acquiring assets that generate consistent cash flow. Rental properties are an excellent choice, but also consider dividend-paying stocks, or even online businesses that produce recurring income. This creates an immediate cash inflow that you can use to either cover living expenses or reinvest into more assets.

2. **Leverage "Good Debt" to Acquire Assets**: While all debt isn't inherently bad, it's important to distinguish between "good" debt and "bad" debt. Good debt is the type of borrowing that helps you acquire an income-generating asset—such as taking out a mortgage to purchase a rental property. If the rent from that property exceeds the mortgage payment, you're using leverage to build wealth. Bad debt, however, is debt taken on to acquire things that don't generate income, such as credit card debt for luxury goods or an expensive car. These kinds of liabilities typically do not generate income and reduce your financial stability.

3. **Invest in Your Financial Education**: Wealthy individuals understand that **knowledge is an asset**. One of the most important assets you can invest in is your own financial education. The more you learn about investing, managing cash flow, and creating wealth, the better equipped you are to make smart decisions. This could involve reading books, taking courses, attending seminars, or finding a mentor.

4. **Automate Savings and Investments**: To consistently build wealth, automate your savings and investment contributions. Set aside a portion of your income to reinvest into assets, making sure that every dollar you earn is either working for you or growing your net worth in some way. This makes wealth-building a habit and ensures you're always increasing your asset base.

The Wealth-Building Mindset: Shift from Consumer to Investor

A huge part of becoming wealthy involves shifting your mindset. Society often encourages us to be consumers—spending money on the latest gadgets, cars, fashion, and experiences. However, to build long-term wealth, you need to think like an investor, not a consumer.

- **Consumers focus on immediate gratification**: Spending money on things that don't generate income (luxury items, cars, expensive vacations) may provide short-term satisfaction, but they don't build long-term wealth.

- **Investors focus on long-term returns**: Investors, on the other hand, make strategic decisions to acquire assets that will appreciate or generate passive income over time. Instead of buying a new car every few years, an investor might put money into real estate or stocks. Instead of buying luxury goods that depreciate, they might invest in a business or an education that can pay dividends for years to come.

The Importance of Managing Liabilities

Reducing and managing liabilities is equally crucial to financial success. While accumulating assets is your primary goal, minimizing liabilities helps ensure that your cash flow remains healthy and that you aren't bogged down by debt. Here are some strategies for managing liabilities effectively:

1. **Pay Down High-Interest Debt First**: Focus on paying off high-interest liabilities like credit cards and personal loans. The interest on these debts can grow quickly, so getting rid of them as soon as possible helps free up money to invest in assets.

2. **Avoid Lifestyle Inflation**: As your income grows, it's easy to fall into the trap of increasing your expenses—

buying a bigger house, a nicer car, or more luxury items. This is called **lifestyle inflation** and can quickly turn into a trap. Instead, make a conscious effort to keep your expenses in check while investing your extra income into assets.

3. **Maintain Low, Controlled Debt**: While some debt (like a mortgage or business loan) can help you build wealth, ensure that any debt you take on is manageable and serves to acquire assets that generate income. Avoid accumulating consumer debt that does not serve this purpose.

4. **Diversify Your Liabilities**: If you must take on debt, try to diversify it. For example, instead of piling everything into a mortgage, consider using business loans to invest in income-producing ventures, or taking out low-interest student loans to increase your earning potential.

Building a Portfolio of Assets: Examples and Strategies for Financial Independence

Building a portfolio of assets is the core of financial independence. A well-diversified portfolio of income-generating assets not only provides steady cash flow but also appreciates over time, allowing you to build wealth that works for you. The more assets you have, the more income streams you create, reducing the reliance on a traditional job or active income. In this chapter, we will explore examples of assets you can create or acquire, and how each of these assets contributes to financial independence.

The Power of a Portfolio Approach

Before we dive into specific asset examples, let's quickly define what a **portfolio of assets** is. A portfolio is a collection of assets that provide a variety of income streams, capital appreciation, and tax advantages. The goal is to build a portfolio that diversifies risk, balances returns, and supports long-term wealth growth.

A well-constructed portfolio combines different types of assets, each contributing to your overall financial goals. The more diversified your portfolio, the less likely a single loss or downturn in one asset class will impact your overall financial health.

Now, let's look at some powerful examples of assets that you can create or acquire to build your portfolio.

---

1. Real Estate (Rental Properties)

What it is: Real estate is one of the most common and reliable assets to create or acquire. This category includes rental properties, commercial real estate, vacation homes, and even land. When done right, real estate can provide passive income through rent payments and long-term capital appreciation as property values increase.

How it generates income:

- **Rental Income**: By purchasing residential or commercial properties, you can rent them out to tenants. The rental income generated on a monthly basis provides a consistent cash flow. The key is to acquire properties where the rental income exceeds the cost of the mortgage, taxes, insurance, and maintenance, creating a positive cash flow.

- **Appreciation**: Over time, properties typically appreciate in value, meaning that the value of the property increases. When you decide to sell, you can sell it for more than you paid, generating capital gains. Real estate markets can fluctuate, but historically, real estate has appreciated steadily over the long term.

How it leads to financial independence: By acquiring multiple rental properties, you can create a growing stream of passive income. With enough properties, your rent payments may cover all your living expenses, allowing you to live without the need for a full-time job. Additionally, if you build equity in the properties over time, you can leverage that equity to acquire even more properties.

---

2. Stocks and Bonds (Equity Investments)

What it is: Stocks and bonds are investments in companies (stocks) or governments/corporations (bonds). Stocks provide ownership in a company, and when the company profits, shareholders typically benefit in the form of dividends or stock price appreciation. Bonds, on the other hand, are a form of debt where you lend money to a company or government, and in return, you earn periodic interest payments.

How it generates income:

- **Dividends**: Many companies distribute a portion of their profits to shareholders in the form of dividends. By purchasing dividend-paying stocks, you receive regular payments, typically quarterly, as long as you hold the stock.

- **Capital Gains**: When the stock price increases, you can sell your shares for a profit. This type of income is realized upon the sale of your stocks but represents an essential part of a long-term wealth-building strategy.

- **Interest from Bonds**: Bonds pay periodic interest, often semi-annually, which is a predictable cash flow. While bonds do not offer the same high growth potential as stocks, they are often more stable and less volatile, making them a solid component of a diversified portfolio.

How it leads to financial independence: Over time, the dividends from stocks and interest from bonds can provide a reliable stream of income. If you reinvest those dividends, you take advantage of compounding, where your earnings generate more earnings. With a sufficiently large stock and bond portfolio, you can create enough passive income to cover your expenses.

---

3. Business Ownership

What it is: Owning a business, whether through an existing company, startup, or franchise, is a powerful way to build wealth. When you own a business, you control its direction, and if successful, it can generate substantial income. Business ownership can take many forms, from owning a local small business to running an online e-commerce platform or a global franchise.

How it generates income:

- **Profits**: As a business owner, the profits from your business operations can be reinvested or used as income. A successful business produces a steady cash flow from sales, services, or products.

- **Sale of the Business**: If the business grows and becomes profitable, it may eventually be sold for a substantial amount of money, providing you with a lump sum capital gain.

How it leads to financial independence: A well-run business can generate income without the need for you to be actively involved in its daily operations, especially if you hire managers and create systems. If the business is structured properly, you can create passive income streams from profits, making it an excellent way to achieve financial freedom. Additionally, the value of a successful business may grow over time, providing both income and capital appreciation.

---

4. Royalties and Intellectual Property

What it is: Intellectual property (IP), such as patents, trademarks, copyrights, and licensing agreements, can be a powerful income-generating asset. If you own IP, you have the right to license it to others, receive royalties from its use, or sell it outright.

How it generates income:

- **Royalties**: If you have a patent, book, song, or invention, you can license it to other businesses or individuals who will pay you royalties for its use. For example, authors receive royalties when their books are sold, and inventors earn royalties when others manufacture and sell their inventions.

- **Licensing**: If you have a trademark or patent, you can license it to companies in exchange for a fee. This is common in industries like technology, fashion, music, and entertainment.

How it leads to financial independence: Royalties and licensing agreements can provide you with a steady stream of passive income. Once the intellectual property is created and the rights are secured, income can flow in for years or even decades, with little to no additional effort on your part. This type of income can be particularly attractive because it can continue for as long as the intellectual property holds value.

5. Peer-to-Peer Lending and Crowdfunding Investments

What it is: Peer-to-peer (P2P) lending allows you to lend money directly to individuals or businesses via online platforms, bypassing traditional banks. In return, you earn interest on your loans. Crowdfunding investments involve pooling capital with other investors to fund a project or business, typically in exchange for equity or revenue sharing.

How it generates income:

- **Interest Payments**: Through P2P lending platforms, you earn interest on the money you lend. Interest rates can vary based on the risk of the borrower, but the returns can be attractive compared to traditional savings accounts.

- **Revenue Sharing**: With crowdfunding, you may receive a share of the business's revenues or profits. In the case of equity crowdfunding, you can also profit from the appreciation of the business's valuation if the business is sold or goes public.

How it leads to financial independence: Both P2P lending and crowdfunding offer passive income opportunities through interest payments and profit-sharing. While the risks are higher (especially with unsecured loans or startups), the returns can be substantial, providing another income stream that can add to your portfolio of assets.

---

6. Commodities and Precious Metals

What it is: Commodities, like gold, silver, oil, and agricultural products, can be an excellent hedge against inflation and a way to diversify your asset portfolio. Precious metals like gold and silver are tangible assets that tend to hold or increase in value over time, especially during periods of economic uncertainty.

How it generates income:

- **Appreciation**: Commodities such as gold often increase in value when the economy is volatile or inflation is rising. By investing in physical commodities, commodity-focused funds, or mining stocks, you can benefit from appreciation.

- **Income from Commodity-Related Assets**: While physical commodities don't produce regular cash flow, you can invest in commodity-related stocks (such as mining companies) that pay dividends or reinvest earnings.

How it leads to financial independence: By adding commodities to your portfolio, you can hedge against inflation and create a more stable financial foundation. Although commodities may not provide regular income like rental properties or dividends, they add diversification and long-term growth potential.

Asset vs. Liability Mindset: How Adopting This Mindset is Crucial for Long-Term Wealth-Building

The distinction between assets and liabilities isn't just a financial concept—it's a mindset that plays a pivotal role in determining your long-term financial success. The way you think about money, spending, investing, and debt shapes the future of your wealth. Adopting an **asset-oriented mindset**—focused on acquiring and accumulating assets—rather than a **liability-oriented mindset**, which centers on consumption and debt, can significantly accelerate your wealth-building journey.

This chapter explores why developing an asset-focused mindset is crucial for financial independence, the difference between an asset and liability mentality, and how shifting your thinking can lead to lasting wealth creation.

The Core of the Asset vs. Liability Mindset

The foundation of the asset vs. liability mindset is how you perceive and prioritize financial decisions. This perspective goes beyond just managing money—it involves how you approach your everyday spending, saving, investing, and even how you see opportunities in life.

- **Asset Mindset**: An asset-oriented mindset focuses on increasing net worth by acquiring things that **appreciate in value** or **generate income**. People with an asset mindset actively seek ways to have money work for them through investments, real estate, businesses, intellectual property, and more. They prioritize long-term financial security and build multiple streams of income.

- **Liability Mindset**: A liability-oriented mindset focuses on **spending money on things that deplete your wealth** over time. People with this mindset often see wealth as something to spend and enjoy today, rather than something to build for the future. They focus on buying things that depreciate in value (like cars, luxury goods, and the latest technology) and may acquire liabilities that weigh down their financial situation, such as high-interest debt.

The key difference is in how you view your financial resources. If you're focused on liabilities, you're essentially working for money, and your wealth is finite. But if you're focused on assets, you're working to create money, and your wealth can grow exponentially.

The Impact of Your Mindset on Financial Growth

Adopting an asset mindset doesn't just impact your personal wealth—it influences your behavior, goals, and how you approach opportunities. Here's how the asset vs. liability mindset directly affects financial growth:

1. Decision-Making and Spending Habits

- **Asset Mindset**: Individuals with an asset mindset make decisions that benefit them long-term. They'll choose to invest in assets (stocks, real estate, businesses) rather than indulge in instant gratification through high-cost, depreciating purchases. For instance, someone with an asset mindset would rather save and invest in a rental property that provides monthly cash flow, rather than spending on a brand-new luxury car that depreciates the moment it's driven off the lot.

- **Liability Mindset**: Those with a liability mindset are often impulsive spenders. They may purchase items on credit, thinking that having more things improves their status or happiness. However, these purchases often lead to financial stress, especially when liabilities like credit card debt and car loans accumulate, taking money out of their pocket without providing future returns.

2. Long-Term Financial Security vs. Short-Term Gratification

- **Asset Mindset**: People who prioritize assets think about the future and are willing to sacrifice short-term pleasures for long-term security. They understand that **delayed gratification**—the willingness to delay spending money on non-essential items—leads to greater wealth in the future. They build their assets over time, often through real estate, stocks, and passive-income businesses, which grow in value or generate income continuously.

- **Liability Mindset**: Those with a liability mindset often act on short-term desires. This mindset thrives on immediate pleasure, without considering how it will affect future financial stability. Individuals who focus on liabilities tend to live paycheck to paycheck, spending more than they earn and accumulating debts that hinder wealth accumulation.

3. Mindset Around Debt

- **Asset Mindset**: Those with an asset mindset see **debt as a tool** for leveraging their wealth-building efforts. For example, they may take out a mortgage to buy an income-producing rental property or use business loans to expand their company. The key is that they use debt strategically, ensuring that the debt they take on is used to acquire assets that generate cash flow or increase in value.

- **Liability Mindset**: Individuals with a liability mindset view debt as a burden. They take on consumer debt (credit cards, auto loans, etc.) that doesn't lead to wealth generation. They tend to prioritize living on credit and borrowing for non-essential purchases, which causes them to pay high interest and further entrench their financial struggles.

4. Building Multiple Streams of Income

- **Asset Mindset**: Those with an asset-oriented mindset understand the importance of having **multiple income streams**. They focus on creating diverse sources of income that don't rely on a job. Whether it's from rental properties, dividend-paying stocks, online businesses, or intellectual property, they work to make money come to them passively.

- **Liability Mindset**: People with a liability mindset typically rely on one primary source of income—usually a paycheck. They may not see the need to diversify their income streams, which leaves them vulnerable to financial setbacks if their job or primary income source is disrupted.

Why the Asset Mindset Leads to Long-Term Wealth-Building

1. Compounding Growth

The asset mindset promotes the idea of building wealth that works for you. **Compounding growth** is one of the most powerful forces in wealth-building. By focusing on acquiring assets that generate income or appreciate over time, you allow your money to grow exponentially. For example, if you invest in dividend-paying stocks, the dividends you receive can be reinvested, increasing the amount of money working for you.

This compounding effect is often much more powerful than working for a paycheck or focusing on liabilities that only deplete your cash flow. When you adopt the asset mindset, you're thinking about how your money can make more money, whether it's through real estate, investments, or income-generating businesses.

2. Financial Independence

The ultimate goal of adopting an asset-focused mindset is to achieve **financial independence**. This is the state where your assets generate enough passive income to cover your living expenses, so you no longer have to rely on earned income (e.g., a salary or hourly wage). Whether it's through rental income, dividends from stocks, or the profits from a business, once your assets are generating sufficient income, you have more control over your time and can focus on what truly matters to you.

The liability mindset, on the other hand, often keeps people in a cycle of living paycheck to paycheck, unable to break free from the necessity of active work. By accumulating and managing assets, you free yourself from the daily grind.

3. Wealth Building in a Recession-Proof Way

When your wealth is tied to assets that generate income (real estate, dividend stocks, businesses), it's more resilient to market fluctuations and recessions. While a liability-oriented mindset may expose you to the risk of high consumer debt and financial instability during a downturn, an asset-focused portfolio can continue to produce income, regardless of external economic conditions.

How to Develop the Asset vs. Liability Mindset

1. Change Your Spending Habits

- **Prioritize Investments Over Consumption**: Before making a large purchase, ask yourself, "Will this asset increase in value or generate income?" Focus on assets that create cash flow, like real estate or investments in stocks. If it's something that depreciates, such as a new car or luxury item, reconsider whether it aligns with your wealth-building goals.

- **Live Below Your Means**: Resist lifestyle inflation. Just because your income increases doesn't mean you should increase your expenses. Instead, use extra income to acquire assets.

2. Educate Yourself About Wealth-Building Strategies

- Educate yourself on what constitutes an asset and how you can strategically acquire and manage assets. Learn about investment vehicles like stocks, bonds, real estate, and businesses, and focus on the ones that suit your financial goals.

3. Shift Your Perspective on Debt

- Understand the difference between **good debt** (debt that helps acquire income-generating assets) and **bad debt** (debt that leads to liabilities or lifestyle purchases). Take on **good debt** strategically, and avoid **bad debt** that drains your resources.

4. Focus on Long-Term Wealth Goals

- Think long-term. Don't be swayed by the desire for immediate gratification. Instead, focus on building wealth through assets that will pay off over time.

Conclusion: Shifting Your Mindset for Long-Term Wealth

Adopting an asset-focused mindset is essential for achieving long-term wealth-building and financial independence. By prioritizing the acquisition of assets that appreciate or generate income, and minimizing liabilities that drain your resources, you set yourself on the path to financial freedom.

Shifting your mindset from liabilities to assets may take time, but it is one of the most powerful transformations you can make in your financial life. By making conscious decisions to build and acquire wealth, rather than consume and acquire debt, you will not only create financial security for yourself but also position yourself to build lasting generational wealth.

CHAPTER 3

MONEY: A BAD MASTER BUT A GOOD SLAVE

When we think about the role of money in our lives, many of us fall into a trap: we let it dictate what we can and cannot do. But what if, instead, we turned that on its head? Imagine a life where money serves you, working quietly in the background, freeing you to focus on your dreams, values, and goals. This is the distinction between money as a master and money as a slave.

The rich understand that money, when harnessed correctly, can be one of the most valuable assets in the pursuit of financial freedom and a fulfilling life. They don't chase money for its own sake, nor do they let it control them; instead, they give it a job. By assigning money a purpose and a direction, they use it to build wealth, grow opportunities, and sustain their passions.

Understanding the Power Dynamic of Money

Money has an undeniable influence over how people live their lives. For those who serve money, every decision revolves around acquiring more of it. They take jobs they don't enjoy, invest in assets they don't understand, and sacrifice time with loved ones, all to chase a currency that ultimately leaves them feeling depleted. Ironically, the harder they chase, the harder it feels to keep up, leading to a life of stress, fear, and scarcity.

Conversely, those who view money as a tool see it as an enabler, not a dictator. They don't rely solely on a paycheck, nor do they allow their bank balance to define their self-worth. They understand that money, like fire, can burn and destroy if left unchecked but can also be harnessed to produce warmth and power if used correctly. This approach reframes money's role, allowing them to remain in control of their choices and work toward genuine independence.

Why Money Should Never Be the Goal

Many people think, "If only I had more money, I'd be happy." Yet history is full of examples of people who accumulated massive wealth but never found true satisfaction. When money becomes the primary objective, people lose sight of their passions, interests, and values. They might end up making choices that contradict their core beliefs or harm their well-being.

On the other hand, those who use money as a tool for something greater experience a deep sense of purpose and satisfaction. They prioritize meaning and fulfillment, with money acting as a supporting player, not the main act. This approach allows them to feel successful not merely because of financial gains but because of the impact and progress they've made toward a life they truly desire.

Making Money Work for You

One of the best ways to make money a "good slave" is to put it to work. Instead of letting it sit idle or spending it on liabilities, the wealthy use money to generate more wealth. Here are some key strategies they employ:

1. **Investing in Assets:** Rather than spending money on fleeting pleasures, they invest in things that grow in value or generate income over time, such as real estate, stocks, and businesses. Each dollar they invest is like planting a seed that, with time, will yield returns and create further opportunities.

2. **Creating Passive Income Streams:** The wealthy build systems that earn money even when they're not actively working. This could include rental properties, royalties, or automated businesses. With passive income, they free up their time to pursue meaningful goals and avoid dependence on a paycheck.

3. **Leveraging Compounding:** Compounding is one of the most powerful concepts in finance. By reinvesting earnings, the wealthy allow their money to grow exponentially over time. Instead of focusing on instant gratification, they value long-term growth, understanding that small, consistent investments can lead to significant wealth over decades.

4. **Being Disciplined with Spending:** Using money effectively means distinguishing between wants and needs. The wealthy often follow strict spending rules, ensuring their resources are used purposefully. They might budget carefully, delay gratification, and assess each purchase's potential long-term impact, ensuring

that every dollar is either spent wisely or put to work for them.

The Mental Shift: From Chasing Money to Creating Value

When people see money as the goal, they often adopt a scarcity mindset, where every financial decision feels like a struggle. But those who make money a tool instead of an end goal adopt a mindset of abundance, focusing on creating value rather than hoarding wealth. They understand that by contributing to others—whether through products, services, or investments—they not only build wealth but also create a positive impact. This shift from chasing money to generating value fosters lasting satisfaction, resilience, and empowerment.

This approach helps cultivate a "money-positive" mindset, where money is seen as a byproduct of value creation rather than something to be coveted or feared. By focusing on value, people are more likely to take calculated risks, seek innovative solutions, and stay adaptable in a rapidly changing world. They recognize that by helping others, they ultimately help themselves, creating a cycle of growth and prosperity.

Key Lessons to Apply

To make money your slave, not your master, consider the following lessons:

1. **Define Your Purpose Beyond Money:** Clarify your "why." What do you truly want in life? Is it freedom, time with family, travel, or the ability to make a difference? By identifying your core purpose, you can align your financial decisions with your true goals.

2. **Let Money Amplify, Not Direct, Your Life:** When you make decisions, don't let money be the sole factor.

Instead, let it amplify your values and intentions. If you value creativity, invest in skills or resources that help you grow in this area. If freedom is essential, prioritize passive income sources.

3. **Reevaluate Your Relationship with Money Regularly:** As you grow and your priorities evolve, so will your relationship with money. Regularly assess your financial goals, habits, and strategies to ensure they align with your current values.

4. **Seek Financial Knowledge and Guidance:** To make money work for you, become financially literate. Learn about investing, budgeting, taxes, and other essentials. Education empowers you to make informed choices and approach money with confidence.

Mastering Money, Not the Other Way Around

Money is a means, not an end. Those who understand this distinction treat money as a tool—a resource to be used strategically to achieve goals and create security. Unfortunately, many people allow money to control their decisions, aspirations, and even their self-worth. But true financial empowerment lies in turning the tables, making money work for you instead of the other way around.

Money as a Servant, Not a Master

When money becomes the focus of our lives, it shapes our decisions and limits our potential. This is because viewing money primarily as a commodity to spend leads to a cycle of endless consumption. Each paycheck is a stopgap, a temporary satisfaction that ends as soon as we're compelled to buy the next item. In this cycle, money dictates choices, enforcing a life of "living paycheck to paycheck."

On the other hand, viewing money as a servant puts us in control. Instead of relying on income to support spending habits, people with a wealth-building mindset channel money into assets—investments, properties, and other value-building resources that work on their behalf. Rather than merely satisfying needs, money becomes an engine for creating more money, building freedom, and empowering future goals.

The Asset Mindset: Money as a Means to Grow Wealth

Wealthy individuals look at money differently than most. To them, it's a tool to acquire assets rather than just a source of cash flow for daily expenses. Here's the distinction:

1. **Income vs. Assets:** Most people think of income as something to spend. But the wealthy see income as an opportunity to acquire assets, such as stocks, real estate, or business ventures. Assets, unlike everyday expenses, generate returns over time, creating a positive feedback loop of growth and security.

2. **The Power of Compounding:** Money invested in assets grows. Through compounding, investments in financial assets increase in value exponentially, meaning every dollar today can be worth many more dollars in the future. This is how wealth grows quietly in the background, even while you sleep.

3. **Risk Management and Diversification:** Those who master money understand that not all assets are created equal. They seek out diversified investments, balancing risk with the potential for reward. This mindset allows them to remain stable even when one

asset might falter, ensuring that their financial foundation stays strong.

Building a Financial Mindset Focused on Growth, Not Consumption

To master money, it's essential to shift from a consumption-focused mindset to a growth-focused one. This requires seeing each dollar as a tool for future opportunity rather than a temporary satisfaction. Here are practical ways to build this mindset:

1. **Reframe Your Spending Habits:** Before spending, ask yourself if this purchase will create lasting value. This doesn't mean denying enjoyment but rather ensuring that your spending reflects your long-term goals.

2. **Develop a Plan for Financial Growth:** Set clear, actionable goals for where you want to be financially in 5, 10, or 20 years. This might include creating a certain level of passive income, saving for significant investments, or achieving financial independence. With a roadmap, each financial decision becomes part of a larger vision.

3. **Prioritize Financial Education:** Financial literacy is essential for making informed decisions. By learning about investing, budgeting, tax strategies, and other core financial principles, you empower yourself to use money effectively and confidently.

The Payoff: Freedom and Empowerment

When money serves you, it becomes a vehicle for freedom rather than a source of stress. By prioritizing assets over expenses, people create the foundation for financial independence. Assets, after all, provide passive income streams, meaning you aren't reliant on a single source of income. This freedom allows people to pursue interests, take risks, and build lives that aren't defined by financial constraints.

Key Takeaways for Mastering Money

1. **Shift Your Perspective from Spending to Investing:** See each dollar as a potential asset, something that can grow, multiply, and serve your goals.

2. **Cultivate Patience and Discipline:** Wealth-building takes time, but each step compounds over time. Embrace a long-term perspective, allowing your investments to grow and mature.

3. **Stay Informed and Flexible:** Financial landscapes change, and those who succeed are those who adapt. Continuously update your knowledge and be willing to refine your strategies as needed.

4. **Let Money Amplify, Not Define, Your Life:** Ultimately, money should support what you value most. It's a tool, not a goal. Define your goals first, then use money as a means to achieve them.

Psychological Shift: Wealthy People View Money as an Instrument to Create More Wealth Rather Than a Reward to Spend Immediately

What makes wealthy individuals different from others isn't just the size of their bank accounts—it's the mindset they bring to each financial decision. For the wealthy, money is an instrument, a tool with one central purpose: to create more wealth. While many people see money as a reward, something to be enjoyed as soon as they earn it, the wealthy know that spending every dollar immediately is a missed opportunity for long-term growth.

In this chapter, we explore the psychological shift required to view money as a means to future wealth rather than as a source of instant gratification. This shift requires two crucial traits: discipline and patience. Building lasting wealth demands that each financial choice is made with careful intent, keeping a larger goal in mind rather than indulging in immediate pleasures.

The Power of Delayed Gratification

One of the core differences between those who accumulate wealth and those who struggle financially is the ability to delay gratification. While it's natural to want to enjoy the fruits of your labor, those with a wealth-building mindset understand that every dollar spent now is a dollar that could instead be invested, compounding and generating returns.

Delayed gratification is not about denying yourself pleasure or living an austere life. Rather, it's about understanding that sacrificing some immediate comforts can lead to greater security and freedom in the long run. This concept applies beyond just financial decisions—it's a mental framework that wealthy individuals carry into all aspects of their lives. They may postpone lavish purchases, choosing instead to use those funds to invest in assets that will ultimately bring them greater returns.

Money as a Seed, Not a Fruit

To understand the mindset of the wealthy, imagine that every dollar is a seed. When planted and nurtured, each seed can grow into something far more valuable than its original form. Money, when invested wisely, has the potential to create more money. But if we treat every dollar like a fruit, consuming it immediately, we lose the chance to see it grow. This seed-versus-fruit analogy highlights a critical concept: the choice between short-term rewards and long-term growth.

By planting seeds—investing in assets, education, or ventures that offer future returns—the wealthy create cycles of continuous growth. Each seed planted today may multiply into a future tree, producing new seeds, more trees, and so on. This approach allows wealth to grow independently, leading to greater financial security and independence over time.

The Importance of Discipline in Financial Choices

Discipline is a cornerstone of wealth building. Those who accumulate wealth don't leave their finances to chance; they approach each decision with clarity and control. Discipline in spending, investing, and budgeting means they can resist the lure of instant gratification and instead allocate money purposefully.

1. **Budgeting and Planning:** Wealthy individuals often adhere to strict budgets, setting limits on their spending to ensure that their money is being directed toward their goals. They prioritize savings and investments, carving out a significant portion of their income for wealth-building activities.

2. **Avoiding Lifestyle Inflation:** As income grows, it's tempting to upgrade one's lifestyle—bigger homes, nicer cars, more luxuries. The wealthy, however, resist this trap. Instead of letting lifestyle costs eat into their newfound wealth, they choose to keep expenses stable, allowing the excess to be invested. This

approach protects them from becoming trapped in a cycle of high expenses, even as their wealth grows.

3. **Investing in Knowledge and Skills:** The wealthy often invest in financial education and self-improvement, recognizing that personal development is one of the most valuable assets. They study markets, learn about different asset classes, and understand financial principles, empowering themselves to make informed decisions.

Patience: The Silent Partner in Wealth Creation

While discipline is crucial, patience is the silent partner that brings wealth-building to fruition. Investments, whether in stocks, real estate, or businesses, take time to grow. Those who seek quick returns often find themselves disappointed, sometimes even incurring losses in their rush for instant wealth.

1. **Long-Term Investing:** Wealthy individuals favor investments that compound over time. They understand that slow and steady growth, although less glamorous, is often more reliable and impactful than chasing immediate gains. Stocks, real estate, and bonds are examples of assets that benefit from the passage of time, increasing in value as they mature.

2. **Allowing Compounding to Work:** Compounding is one of the most powerful concepts in finance. By reinvesting returns, individuals can experience exponential growth over time. The wealthy understand this concept and allow their money to remain invested, letting compounding do the heavy lifting. This patience allows their wealth to grow in a

way that wouldn't be possible if they frequently withdrew or spent their returns.

3. **Staying the Course:** Economic downturns, market fluctuations, and financial crises are inevitable. Wealthy individuals develop the patience to weather these storms, trusting in their long-term strategy. By holding steady, they avoid impulsive actions, maintaining their investments through both highs and lows.

Transforming Money from a Reward into a Resource

When money is seen as a reward, it becomes something to be consumed, something that loses its value once spent. But when money is viewed as a resource, it becomes an asset that can continue to work indefinitely. This transformation in mindset empowers individuals to take control of their financial future. Instead of seeking short-lived satisfaction, they seek financial security, independence, and the ability to pursue their passions without financial limitations.

This shift in perspective requires practice and conscious effort. It involves questioning ingrained beliefs about money, developing financial literacy, and building a lifestyle that prioritizes purpose over impulse. With time, this approach becomes a habit, leading to stronger financial health and a sense of empowerment.

Practical Steps to Develop the Wealth Mindset

1. **Define Clear Financial Goals:** Knowing what you want to achieve with your wealth will help you stay disciplined. Define specific goals for savings, investments, and passive income streams, and create actionable steps toward reaching them.

2. **Set Boundaries on Spending:** A disciplined approach to spending requires limits. Create a budget that balances your needs and wants, but always ensures that a portion of your income goes toward wealth-building.

3. **Seek Out Financial Mentors or Education:** If you're unsure how to manage money, don't hesitate to seek guidance. Learning from experienced investors or educators can provide valuable insights and strategies.

4. **Commit to a Long-Term Perspective:** Remind yourself regularly that wealth-building is a marathon, not a sprint. Celebrate small milestones along the way, but keep your eye on the larger goal of financial freedom and stability.

Conclusion

Building wealth isn't about luck or shortcuts; it's about discipline, patience, and a fundamental psychological shift. By viewing money as a tool rather than a reward, wealthy individuals take control of their financial futures, channeling each dollar toward lasting growth and security. This mindset shift empowers them to make decisions rooted in their goals, their values, and their dreams, ultimately leading to a life where money works for them—not the other way around.

CHAPTER 4

THE ART OF CAPITALISM AND MAKING MONEY FROM MONEY

The philosophy of capitalism is rooted in the ideals of freedom, individual responsibility, and the pursuit of personal interests as a means to contribute to collective prosperity. At its core, capitalism is based on the notion that individuals, when given the freedom to pursue their own economic interests, can create wealth and innovations that benefit society as a whole. This philosophy emphasizes voluntary exchange, private ownership, and the efficient allocation of resources through market forces rather than central planning.

Key Principles of Capitalist Philosophy

1. **Individual Freedom and Choice**
   Capitalism is grounded in the belief that individuals should have the liberty to make choices about their work, investments, and consumption. This freedom to choose is considered essential to personal autonomy

and fulfillment, allowing people to pursue careers, create businesses, and invest in ways that align with their values, skills, and ambitions.

2. **Private**   **Property**
   Private property rights are foundational to capitalism, as they provide individuals with the security to own and control assets. Ownership encourages responsibility, incentivizes maintenance and improvement, and offers individuals the ability to use their property to generate wealth. This principle also encourages innovation, as creators can reap the benefits of their inventions and ideas.

3. **Competition**   **and**   **Innovation**
   In a capitalist system, competition acts as a self-regulating mechanism that drives efficiency, innovation, and quality. When businesses compete, they strive to meet consumer needs in better, faster, and more cost-effective ways, pushing the boundaries of technology and service. This competition benefits society by leading to a broader array of products, services, and solutions to various needs and problems.

4. **Voluntary**   **Exchange**
   The principle of voluntary exchange asserts that economic transactions should be conducted freely between consenting parties. Each party in a transaction does so because they believe it will benefit them. This creates a self-reinforcing system of trade where value is created on both sides, as each participant receives something they value more than what they gave up.

5. **Profit**   **as**   **a**   **Measure**   **of**   **Value**
   In capitalism, profit is seen as a measure of value

created. When a business makes a profit, it typically indicates that it has provided something of value to its customers, efficiently managed resources, and compensated its workers. Profit serves as an incentive for businesses to innovate, expand, and better serve customers, which can lead to societal advancement through new products, technologies, and services.

6. **Minimal Government Intervention**
   While capitalism acknowledges a role for government—such as ensuring rule of law, enforcing contracts, and protecting property rights—its philosophy generally favors minimal intervention. The belief is that free markets are the most effective means of allocating resources, as opposed to government-directed or centrally planned economies. Minimal interference allows markets to adjust naturally to supply, demand, and innovation without artificial constraints that may hinder growth.

The Role of Capitalism in Human Flourishing

At its best, capitalism is viewed as a system that empowers individuals to achieve self-fulfillment, success, and independence through their own efforts. By enabling people to pursue their unique talents and ambitions, capitalism is seen as contributing to human flourishing, allowing individuals the opportunity to reach their full potential.

Capitalism is not merely an economic system but a broader worldview that regards human beings as capable, self-reliant, and deserving of freedom in their economic lives. By emphasizing personal responsibility, it promotes a mindset in which individuals are encouraged to take control of their destinies, contribute to society through their talents, and create value for others.

Critics of Capitalism and Counterarguments

While capitalism promotes growth and freedom, it has been critiqued for sometimes creating inequality and fostering excessive consumerism. Critics argue that it can lead to disparities in wealth and access to resources, placing significant power in the hands of the wealthy. Supporters, however, argue that capitalism, when combined with social safety nets and ethical business practices, can address many of these challenges. They suggest that capitalism's flexibility allows for adaptation to changing societal needs, promoting both economic freedom and, when well-regulated, fairer distributions of wealth.

Capitalism's Role in Wealth Creation

At its core, capitalism is a system that provides individuals with the freedom to create wealth, not merely through labor but by investing in and owning assets. In contrast to systems that primarily reward labor with wages, capitalism empowers people to gain financial leverage by owning things that can appreciate in value or generate income on their own. The wealthy understand this principle deeply, as they use capitalism's framework to multiply their wealth in ways that do not require trading time for money.

Under capitalism, individuals have the autonomy to invest in various assets, from stocks and real estate to businesses and intellectual property, each with the potential to appreciate in value or provide passive income streams. This focus on asset creation and investment, rather than just working for wages, is at the heart of wealth accumulation. While wages are typically taxed heavily and limited by time and energy constraints, returns on investments benefit from a favorable tax structure in many countries, compounding their growth.

The Concept of Making Money from Money

For many, money is simply the means to buy necessities and comforts; for the wealthy, it is a powerful tool that can be used to generate more wealth. When money is actively invested rather than spent, it has the potential to grow through dividends, interest, or capital gains. This is the essence of making money from money, a foundational practice in wealth building.

By creating a portfolio of diverse investments, individuals reduce their dependency on earned income and allow their capital to work for them. Capital gains in real estate, for instance, can produce returns in the form of rental income or appreciation in property value. Similarly, investments in the stock market can yield dividends and increase in market value over time, creating wealth with little direct effort from the investor. This approach emphasizes the importance of letting money work autonomously rather than being actively earned through labor.

The Benefits of Asset Ownership

Ownership is a powerful concept in capitalism, allowing people to hold and control valuable resources, whether tangible (like real estate) or intangible (like intellectual property or shares in a company). Each asset class brings unique benefits:

1. **Real Estate:** Real estate has long been a wealth builder due to its potential for appreciation and income generation. Owners can earn rental income while also benefitting from the property's increase in value over time. Real estate is a tangible asset, often perceived as a safe investment due to its physical presence and historical appreciation trends.

2. **Stocks and Bonds:** Stocks represent ownership in companies, while bonds are debt instruments issued by corporations or governments. By investing in stocks, individuals can participate in a company's growth and profits without directly managing operations. Bonds, on the other hand, provide fixed-income returns. Both stocks and bonds offer relatively accessible entry points for those looking to build wealth through investment.

3. **Businesses and Entrepreneurship:** Owning a business provides direct control over wealth generation. While it involves risk and effort, the rewards can be substantial, as business ownership provides income and asset value growth. Many wealthy individuals have accumulated significant wealth by founding or acquiring businesses, as the returns on a successful venture can far exceed those of traditional investments.

4. **Intellectual Property:** In today's knowledge-based economy, intellectual property (IP) can be incredibly valuable. IP assets, such as patents, trademarks, and copyrights, create opportunities for recurring income from licensing or royalties. They are increasingly significant for those in fields like technology, entertainment, and publishing, where intellectual work is monetized.

Compounding Wealth through Reinvestment

One of capitalism's greatest benefits is the ability to compound wealth. This occurs when returns are reinvested, creating a cycle of exponential growth. The wealthy capitalize on this principle by allowing their returns to remain within their investments, reinvesting dividends and capital gains back into their portfolios. Over time, compounding can produce significant returns, even from modest initial investments.

Reinvestment amplifies growth by continually adding to the base of assets, creating a snowball effect. For example, when dividends from stocks are reinvested, the investor increases their ownership stake in the company, allowing for even greater returns in the future. Real estate investors who reinvest rental income into additional properties expand their portfolio, creating multiple income streams. This continuous reinvestment separates the wealthy from those who merely save, as it accelerates wealth accumulation without requiring additional labor.

Financial Independence Through Capitalism

By focusing on creating wealth from investments rather than labor alone, individuals can achieve financial independence. Capitalism provides the framework for this transformation, empowering people to harness their assets as wealth generators. Unlike wage earners, who are often reliant on a single income stream, those who invest in assets enjoy greater financial resilience and independence.

Financial independence is reached when passive income from investments meets or exceeds living expenses. With a diversified portfolio, an individual can gain freedom from financial worry, as their money works for them rather than relying on constant labor. For many wealthy individuals, this is the ultimate goal: achieving financial freedom, which allows them to pursue passions and interests without being limited by the need for a paycheck.

The Wealthy Mindset Toward Capitalism

The wealthy embrace capitalism not merely as a system of ownership but as an art form, carefully selecting and cultivating their investments to maximize returns. For them, capitalism is not a race to earn and spend but a disciplined strategy for long-term wealth generation. They view their capital as an employee—a force that can work tirelessly around the clock, provided it's invested wisely.

To maximize the benefits of capitalism, wealthy individuals often adopt a long-term perspective, understanding that wealth takes time to grow. They remain patient, allowing their investments to compound, often weathering market downturns with the confidence that, in the long run, their assets will recover and continue to appreciate. This mindset—focusing on asset growth rather than immediate gratification—is crucial for building lasting wealth within a capitalist framework.

Money-Making Mechanisms: How the Wealthy Multiply Their Money

For the wealthy, money is not just a resource for spending but a powerful tool for generating more wealth. By strategically investing in income-generating assets, they create and grow their wealth with minimal need for ongoing labor. Let's explore some of the primary money-making mechanisms used by the wealthy—from real estate and stocks to entrepreneurship—with examples to illustrate each approach.

1. Real Estate: Building Wealth through Property

Real estate has long been a favorite investment avenue for the wealthy, largely because it combines the potential for capital appreciation with the possibility of regular income. Wealthy investors purchase properties with the intention of benefiting from both rising property values over time and income from tenants.

- **Example: Rental   Properties**
  A wealthy individual buys an apartment building in a growing urban area. Each month, tenants pay rent, providing the owner with a steady income stream. Additionally, as property values rise, the building's market price appreciates, allowing the investor to sell it later at a profit or refinance to access funds for new investments.

This dual benefit of rental income and long-term appreciation is what makes real estate so appealing. In some cases, investors take it a step further by renovating properties to increase their value, allowing them to charge higher rents and secure greater profits upon resale.

- **Example: Commercial   Real   Estate**
  Investors often acquire commercial properties such as office buildings, retail spaces, or industrial warehouses. For instance, a wealthy investor might purchase a retail center and lease space to various businesses. Because commercial leases often last several years, they provide stable, predictable income. Moreover, companies often pay higher rents than residential tenants, making commercial real estate especially lucrative for seasoned investors.

2. Stocks: Owning a Share of Profits and Growth

Stocks offer a way for investors to own a small piece of a company and benefit from its growth. Through stock ownership, the wealthy earn returns both from stock price appreciation and dividends, which many companies distribute to shareholders from their profits.

- **Example: Long-Term Stock Investments**
  Wealthy investors often hold onto stocks of established companies like Apple, Microsoft, or Coca-Cola, which have strong historical performance and reliable dividend payments. For example, if someone bought shares of Apple in 2010, their investment would have grown significantly as the company's stock price skyrocketed over the years. Meanwhile, dividend payments provide a steady income stream, which many wealthy investors reinvest to compound their returns.

- **Example: Dividend Investing**
  Some investors focus on dividend-paying stocks for steady, passive income. A wealthy investor might buy shares in companies like Johnson & Johnson or Procter & Gamble, known for consistently high dividends. Even in volatile markets, dividend stocks often remain resilient, making them a popular choice for those seeking stable income along with capital growth.

3. Entrepreneurship: Building and Scaling Businesses

Entrepreneurship provides perhaps the most direct and potentially lucrative way to generate wealth. Through business ownership, individuals can create a stream of income from the profits their companies generate. For the wealthy, entrepreneurship is not just a career choice; it's a primary wealth-building strategy.

- **Example: Starting a Successful Company**
  A well-known example is Elon Musk, who co-founded companies like PayPal, Tesla, and SpaceX. By identifying opportunities in e-commerce, electric vehicles, and space technology, Musk created enormous value. Tesla, for instance, grew from a small

electric vehicle company into a global leader in renewable energy, and Musk's net worth rose exponentially as the company's valuation soared. This level of wealth generation is possible only through successful entrepreneurship, where founders benefit not only from salaries but also from the vast appreciation of their company's stock.

- **Example:**   **Franchising**
Some entrepreneurs build wealth through franchising. Ray Kroc, the man behind McDonald's expansion, grew the business into one of the largest franchises in the world. He realized the potential of scaling through franchising, allowing him to build a global fast-food empire with steady, consistent cash flow from franchise fees and royalties. Franchising can also be done on a smaller scale, where wealthy individuals invest in a popular franchise, benefiting from an established brand and proven business model without starting from scratch.

4. Private Equity and Venture Capital: Profiting from Business Growth

Through private equity and venture capital, wealthy investors finance early-stage or growing companies, allowing them to capture significant returns if the businesses succeed. These types of investments can yield high rewards, but they come with substantial risk, as many startups and private companies fail.

- **Example: Venture   Capital   Investments**
Venture capitalists like Peter Thiel, an early investor in Facebook, have made fortunes by funding startups in their early stages. Thiel's initial investment of $500,000 in Facebook turned into over $1 billion

when the company went public. By providing capital to promising companies, venture capitalists capture exponential returns when these companies grow and either get acquired or go public.

- **Example: Private Equity Buyouts** Private equity firms purchase struggling or undervalued companies, make strategic improvements, and sell them at a profit. For instance, a private equity firm might acquire a family-owned manufacturing company, streamline operations, and improve profitability before selling it to a larger conglomerate. The returns from these deals can be substantial, as the firm benefits from both improved earnings and the sale's premium price.

5. Alternative Investments: Diversifying Wealth

Beyond traditional assets like stocks, real estate, and businesses, the wealthy often invest in alternative assets such as commodities, art, and collectibles. These investments offer diversification and serve as hedges against economic downturns, as they often perform differently from mainstream investments.

- **Example: Art and Collectibles** Wealthy individuals might purchase valuable artwork, rare coins, or vintage cars. These assets tend to appreciate over time, especially if they are unique or have historical significance. For instance, a rare Picasso painting or a classic Ferrari can increase in value significantly over decades. When sold, these collectibles can generate substantial returns, making them appealing long-term investments.

- **Example: Commodities and Precious Metals**
  Some investors diversify their portfolios by purchasing commodities like gold, silver, or oil, which often perform well during economic uncertainty. For example, during times of inflation, gold often retains or increases in value, protecting an investor's wealth. Precious metals are thus a popular store of value for the wealthy who seek to preserve their assets against inflationary pressures.

6. Fixed-Income Investments: Stability and Predictability

While stocks and real estate offer high returns, wealthy investors also look for stability through fixed-income assets like bonds and certificates of deposit (CDs). Although these investments may offer lower returns, they provide predictable income and are typically lower risk, making them ideal for preserving capital.

- **Example: Municipal Bonds**
  Wealthy investors often invest in municipal bonds, which are issued by local governments to fund public projects. These bonds are attractive not only because they provide regular interest payments but also because the interest income is often exempt from federal and, in some cases, state taxes. A high-net-worth individual might invest in a portfolio of municipal bonds to generate tax-free income while preserving their capital.

Real-Life Example: From Earning to Creating Wealth

Let me share a personal experience that really opened my eyes to the power of creating wealth through assets, rather than just earning a salary.

A friend of mine worked as a private school tutor, earning $15,000 annually for 6 hours of work a day. While the salary was decent, it was still a traditional "work-for-money" setup, where their income was tied directly to the hours spent tutoring. The more they worked, the more they earned, but once their hours were maxed out, so was their income. There was no room to scale beyond that limit, and to earn more, they would have to sacrifice their free time, which created a ceiling on their financial growth.

I, on the other hand, started my journey by working for money—saving up to build some capital. Once I had enough, I decided to invest in renting out wood cabins. I acquired several cabins at $500 per month each. The cabins were in a desirable location, and I rented them out for $1,500 per month.

Here's the beauty of this setup: once the cabins were rented out, I no longer had to trade time for money. The cabins became a source of passive income. The rent I received—$1,500 per month for each cabin—was essentially creating money for me. I could spend my time focusing on other ventures, enjoying life, or even reinvesting in additional properties.

In the end, this process allowed me to generate more money than my friend's salary, without any active work on my part. I wasn't limited by hours or the need to constantly trade time for money. The more cabins I rented out, the more money I made. The capital I invested worked for me, multiplying itself over time.

This experience was a powerful lesson in how owning income-generating assets, like real estate, can be a far more effective strategy for wealth accumulation than relying on earned income. It's a system that rewards smart investments and patience, rather than hours worked. Through this process, I realized that true wealth is created not just by earning money, but by finding ways to let money work for you.

CHAPTER 5

WHY A JOB IS A SHORT-TERM SOLUTION TO A LONG-TERM PROBLEM

In the grand theater of human existence, where time is our most finite resource, we are all cast in roles defined by our need to survive, prosper, and ultimately leave a legacy. The pursuit of money—while deeply personal and varied—often begins with a seemingly simple solution: get a job. It's the entry point for the vast majority of people seeking financial stability. But upon closer inspection, we begin to see that the job, in all its promise of security, may not be the answer to life's deeper questions. It is, perhaps, a necessary step in a broader journey, but it is not the destination.

At first glance, the job seems like the epitome of practicality. It offers a direct exchange: your time and skills for money. The contract is clear, and the benefits, immediate. But the job, in all its routine and predictability, is a temporary fix for an enduring problem. It offers the illusion of security but fails to address the underlying issue—our relationship with time, wealth, and our purpose in life.

Philosophically speaking, the job is a reaction to the finite nature of existence. We all face the constraints of time and the need for survival. A job is often the first response to this human predicament. But as we become more attuned to the complexities of the world, we begin to see that a job is simply a temporary solution to a much deeper, more existential challenge: how do we free ourselves from the perpetual cycle of exchanging time for money, so that we can live in a way that is fulfilling, meaningful, and ultimately, prosperous?

The true issue lies not in the job itself, but in the mindset that surrounds it. A job—while necessary—often reinforces a belief system that traps us into viewing time as something to be sold, not invested. It subtly encourages the idea that our value is tied solely to the hours we clock in and the effort we put out. In doing so, it distracts us from the higher pursuit of wealth: wealth not only in money, but in time, freedom, and the ability to shape our destiny.

The long-term problem we face, then, is not simply one of financial survival, but one of self-empowerment and control over our most precious resource: time. A job, while offering a steady paycheck, limits our capacity to truly engage with the world in a way that fosters growth and creativity. It is not a bad solution, but it is limited in its scope. To solve the long-term problem, we must shift our thinking from viewing jobs as the ultimate answer to seeing them as a tool—one that can be used wisely, but not relied upon indefinitely.

As we move forward in this chapter, we will explore the ways in which the job is not the final answer to our financial and existential questions, but rather a stepping stone toward something greater: the pursuit of wealth that frees us from the constraints of time and enables us to create a lasting impact on the world.

Limitations of Salaries: Jobs Offer Stability but Are Limited in Wealth-Building Potential

While a salaried job offers undeniable stability, it comes with inherent limitations that restrict its potential as a long-term wealth-building strategy. This limitation isn't about the job's value or the work it requires—it's about the fundamental structure of the salary itself. A salary is a form of active income, meaning that the money you earn is directly tied to the hours you work, your output, or your position. As such, the earning potential is capped in a way that makes it difficult to build substantial wealth over time.

1. The Cap on Earnings: Why Time Limits Wealth

The most glaring limitation of a salaried job is that it operates on a fixed exchange rate—your time for money. No matter how hard you work or how skilled you become, there is a point at which your salary plateaus. Even with promotions or raises, your income is still tethered to the number of hours you can physically work or the salary band your job dictates. In essence, your earning capacity is finite, bound by the hours in a day and the limits of the salary structure within your company or industry.

At some point, you hit a ceiling. There's only so much you can work in a day, and no matter how much your boss values you or how much extra effort you put in, there's an upper limit to the amount of money you can earn. This cap becomes even more apparent as you rise through the ranks. Executives or professionals in high-paying roles are certainly better compensated, but they still trade large chunks of their time for money, limiting their ability to accumulate wealth at the rate they could through other means.

2. The Cost of Time: How the Job Keeps You Busy but Not Rich

When you work for a salary, you're essentially exchanging your time for money, and time is a resource that can't be replenished. Each hour spent working for a paycheck is an hour you're not spending on activities that could create wealth without direct effort. This makes a salaried job a relatively slow and inefficient way to build lasting wealth.

Think of it this way: If you work 40 hours a week, that's 2,080 hours a year (assuming you take a few weeks off for vacation). If you're earning $50,000 a year, your hourly rate is about $24 an hour. But if you want to significantly increase your wealth, you'll need to find ways to earn money beyond the hours you spend working. Passive income—whether through investments, business ventures, or other income-generating assets—allows for wealth to grow exponentially, without increasing the number of hours you work. A salaried job doesn't provide this leverage.

3. Job Security: A Double-Edged Sword

One of the most common arguments in favor of a salaried job is the sense of job security it provides. Having a steady paycheck can bring peace of mind, particularly during economic uncertainty. But the irony here is that while the job may offer stability, it often ties your personal and financial security to the fortunes of someone else—your employer. You're not in control of your income growth. A company can downsize, restructure, or change its priorities, and in many cases, your job can be taken away regardless of how hard you work or how committed you are.

In contrast, wealth built through assets such as investments, real estate, or businesses provides more control over your income. It's not subject to the whims of an employer, and its potential for growth isn't tied to a clock-in or clock-out timecard. Instead, the income generated by these assets can continue to grow, even when you're not actively working, offering a kind of financial independence and security that a job simply can't.

4. Active Income vs. Passive Income: The Difference That Matters

A job provides what is called active income. Active income is earned through direct involvement and effort. When you're employed, you must show up, perform tasks, and exert energy to get paid. There is no way to earn more money unless you work more hours, take on more responsibilities, or negotiate a higher salary.

This is in stark contrast to passive income, where the money you earn is generated by investments or systems that require little or no ongoing effort from you once they are set up. Examples of passive income include dividends from stocks, rental income from properties, or profits from businesses you own but don't run day-to-day. With passive income, your money works for you, rather than you working for it.

As long as you remain in the realm of salaried employment, you are bound by the limitations of active income. It requires your direct participation, and thus, your earning potential is intrinsically tied to the finite nature of your time. No matter how hard you work, it's impossible to generate true wealth through active income alone.

5. Inflation and Rising Living Costs: How Salaries Lag Behind

Another limitation of salaried income is its vulnerability to inflation and the rising cost of living. While wages may increase incrementally over time, they often fail to keep pace with inflation, meaning that the purchasing power of your salary can erode over the long term. For example, a salary that seems generous today may be less so in 10 or 20 years if inflation outpaces wage growth.

In contrast, wealth built through assets like real estate, stocks, or businesses tends to appreciate over time. These assets don't just keep up with inflation—they can outpace it, growing in value and generating returns that keep your wealth ahead of the curve. In this way, a job's salary is not just limited in its wealth-building potential; it's also limited by the broader economic forces that diminish the real value of your earnings.

6. The Trap of Comfort: Settling into Mediocrity

Perhaps one of the most subtle but pervasive limitations of a salaried job is how it can create a sense of complacency. The stability and predictability that come with a job can lull you into a sense of comfort, making you less likely to take risks or seek out new opportunities. As time goes on, many individuals find themselves stuck in the cycle of working for a paycheck, unable to break free and explore other ways of generating wealth or achieving their goals.

In contrast, those who take a more entrepreneurial approach to wealth-building—whether through investing, owning businesses, or creating income streams that don't require constant effort—are continually challenged to think outside the box, take calculated risks, and seek out innovative solutions to financial growth. The job, by its nature, doesn't encourage this kind of thinking. It encourages a "safe" and predictable existence, but one that limits your true wealth potential.

Conclusion: The Salary as a Stepping Stone, Not a Solution

A job, with its stable paycheck and predictable routine, offers a critical foundation for those just starting out in life, or those in need of immediate financial security. However, relying solely on a salary as a means of wealth-building is like trying to fill a well with a spoon. It's a limited tool in a broader journey toward financial independence and lasting wealth.

To build substantial wealth, we must recognize the inherent limitations of salaried employment and explore other avenues that provide passive income, leverage, and the potential for exponential growth. Jobs may offer stability, but it is the pursuit of investments, businesses, and assets that will provide the freedom and wealth we seek for the long term.

The Financial Trap of a Job: Working Solely for a Paycheck Often Restricts People from Experiencing the Financial Freedom They Desire

The pursuit of a steady paycheck is a path many people choose for the security it brings. After all, a job provides a reliable source of income, predictable work hours, and, for some, a sense of fulfillment. However, while jobs are often necessary stepping stones in life, relying solely on a paycheck can lead to what's known as the "financial trap." This trap restricts people from achieving the financial freedom they desire, keeping them in a cycle of dependency on their paycheck and limiting their potential to grow real wealth.

The trap lies in the way a job structures not just income, but also time, lifestyle, and ultimately, a person's financial perspective. When all efforts are directed at maintaining a steady paycheck, it becomes easy to overlook broader financial opportunities and to settle into a pattern that prioritizes short-term stability over long-term growth.

1. Dependency on a Single Income Stream: The Risk of Putting All Eggs in One Basket

One of the main pitfalls of working solely for a paycheck is the reliance on a single source of income. With only one income stream, your financial well-being is dependent entirely on your employer and your ability to maintain employment. While jobs can offer stability, they are not immune to external risks—economic downturns, company restructuring, automation, and other forces outside an employee's control.

This dependency on a single income is inherently risky, as it leaves people vulnerable to layoffs, pay cuts, and changes in the job market. Unlike diversified income sources—such as investments, rental properties, or side businesses—a single paycheck is a narrow foundation on which to build financial security. Should that paycheck disappear, many are left with limited options and no safety net, which restricts their sense of financial freedom.

2. The Time-for-Money Trap: Limited by Hours Worked

The traditional job structure is built on the concept of exchanging time for money. Employees are paid based on the hours they work, whether salaried or hourly, which means their income is directly tied to the time they invest. This arrangement inherently limits how much a person can earn, as there are only so many hours in a day, and only so much energy a person can expend.

This "time-for-money" model restricts the potential for wealth growth because it doesn't allow money to grow independently of time. True financial freedom often comes from generating income that isn't tied to hours worked, allowing people to earn even while they sleep. In contrast, when income is directly tied to time, it becomes nearly impossible to break free from the cycle of working for a paycheck.

For example, consider two people: one who works a 40-hour job and earns a steady income, and another who, in addition to a job, has investments in real estate or stocks. While the first person's earnings are capped by the hours they can work, the second person has income sources that grow over time, requiring little to no active effort. The financial trap of a paycheck restricts people to active income, preventing them from experiencing the exponential growth potential that comes from passive income.

3. Lifestyle Inflation: How a Job Can Create a Spending Trap

One of the lesser-discussed aspects of relying on a paycheck is the way it often fuels lifestyle inflation. Lifestyle inflation occurs when a person's expenses rise in tandem with their income. As people earn more from raises, bonuses, or promotions, they often increase their spending on bigger homes, nicer cars, and luxury items. While there's nothing inherently wrong with improving one's quality of life, this kind of spending doesn't build wealth—it keeps people locked in the financial trap of living paycheck to paycheck.

In fact, lifestyle inflation can lead people to feel like they're constantly "needing" their job to maintain their standard of living, creating dependency on that paycheck. This dependency erodes the potential for financial freedom, as any job loss or income change would severely impact their ability to sustain their lifestyle. Instead of investing or saving their additional income, people trapped by lifestyle inflation simply consume it, leaving them no closer to true financial independence.

4. Lack of Financial Growth: The Job's Limited Wealth-Building Potential

Another element of the financial trap is the limited potential for wealth growth through a job alone. While promotions, raises, and bonuses can boost earnings, they rarely create the kind of wealth that grows independently over time. Even in high-paying professions, the accumulation of wealth remains bound by the limits of salary increases, which are typically incremental and subject to inflationary erosion.

Real wealth-building requires assets that appreciate over time—investments, businesses, real estate, or ventures with compounding returns. A paycheck does not have this compounding power, meaning that people working solely for a salary miss out on the exponential growth opportunities available through asset accumulation. By focusing only on earning more from their job, they delay or miss the chance to create lasting wealth through other financial vehicles.

5. The Illusion of Stability: False Security in a Paycheck

A steady paycheck often creates a false sense of security. It can feel like a safeguard, protecting you from financial hardship. However, this stability is conditional and dependent on factors beyond the employee's control. Jobs are subject to economic fluctuations, company decisions, and technological changes that can instantly alter someone's employment status. Those who rely solely on a paycheck may not realize how fragile this stability truly is until it's too late.

In contrast, wealth generated through diversified assets—whether investments in stocks, real estate, or businesses—offers a form of security that doesn't rely on a single source.

By creating income streams that function independently of a job, individuals gain more control over their financial future and reduce the vulnerability associated with paycheck dependency. This is true financial freedom, which can be achieved only by stepping outside the confines of a job-based income.

6. The Cost of Dreams Deferred: How Paychecks Limit Personal Goals

Perhaps one of the greatest costs of working solely for a paycheck is the limitation it places on personal goals and dreams. The security of a job often makes people defer their dreams, whether it's starting a business, traveling the world, or pursuing a passion project. When people are locked into the cycle of working for a paycheck, they may feel unable to take the financial risks necessary to explore these opportunities.

By focusing on the paycheck as the sole source of income, people often sacrifice years or even decades in pursuit of security, delaying personal goals and dreams that could enrich their lives in ways beyond money. True financial freedom allows people the choice to pursue their goals without being bound by financial constraints. When income is diversified and not entirely reliant on a job, it's easier to take risks, explore passions, and create a life that aligns with personal values and aspirations.

Importance of Creating Money: How Passive Income Unlocks Financial Security and Independence

In the journey to financial security, a profound shift occurs when people move from merely earning money to *creating* money. This shift is marked by the pursuit of passive income—money generated by assets that continue to earn independently of one's active work. Passive income, often derived from investments, real estate, or businesses, is a form of self-sustaining wealth that provides freedom from the traditional constraints of a salary-based income. When people create money through assets, they step out of the limited cycle of trading time for money and into a realm where financial security and independence become possible.

The importance of creating money goes beyond the accumulation of wealth. It represents a fundamental shift in financial philosophy, where money is seen not just as a means to cover expenses but as a tool to build a life of freedom, flexibility, and choice. In this chapter, we'll explore why creating passive income is vital, and how it provides a pathway to financial independence that is simply unattainable through salary-based income alone.

1. The Freedom from Time Constraints: How Passive Income Liberates Your Schedule

One of the most powerful aspects of passive income is that it's not tied to time in the same way a salary is. When people work for a paycheck, they exchange hours of their lives for money. This model, while effective in the short term, is inherently limited by the finite nature of time. People can only work so many hours in a day, and as a result, their earning potential is capped.

In contrast, passive income provides a means to earn money without direct involvement or continuous effort. Investments such as dividend stocks, rental properties, or income-generating businesses allow money to grow and accumulate without the need for constant oversight. This freedom from time constraints not only expands earning potential but also frees individuals to pursue their passions, spend time with loved ones, or engage in activities that contribute to personal growth and fulfillment.

Passive income transforms the way we approach wealth-building. It's not about clocking in more hours, but about creating assets that work on their own, allowing people to break free from the rigid structure of traditional employment and the pressure of working endlessly to make ends meet.

2. Financial Security: The Stability of Diversified Income Streams

Relying solely on a paycheck can be precarious. Jobs come with built-in instability: they are subject to layoffs, economic downturns, and changes in company policy. When people rely entirely on a single income source, they put their financial stability in the hands of forces outside their control.

Creating passive income through assets changes this equation by diversifying income streams. For instance, someone with a mix of rental income, stock dividends, and a small online business is less vulnerable to financial stress if one source of income experiences a downturn. This diversification acts as a financial buffer, providing security against unexpected events that might otherwise disrupt a paycheck-dependent lifestyle.

By building passive income streams, people gain a foundation of financial stability. This stability fosters a sense of security that goes beyond what a paycheck can offer, as it is not subject to the same risks and limitations. Creating money through diversified assets allows individuals to weather economic changes with resilience and confidence.

3. The Compounding Effect: Why Passive Income Builds Wealth Faster

One of the most remarkable qualities of passive income is its ability to compound over time, leading to exponential growth. When people invest in assets like stocks, real estate, or businesses, these assets often appreciate in value or yield returns that increase year over year. Unlike a salary, which typically grows incrementally through raises or promotions, passive income has the potential to grow exponentially due to the power of compounding.

For example, an investment in dividend stocks doesn't just provide regular payouts; the dividends can be reinvested, allowing the original investment to grow and yield even more dividends over time. Similarly, rental properties may increase in value, and rental income can rise in parallel with market trends. Compounding enables people to grow wealth faster than they would through salary increases alone, as money itself begins to work as an independent engine of growth.

The compounding effect is one of the key advantages of creating money rather than simply earning it. By building wealth through assets that appreciate and generate returns over time, people can achieve a level of financial growth that far surpasses what is possible within a salary structure. This wealth-building power allows for faster accumulation of assets, accelerating the path to financial independence.

4. Independence from Economic Cycles: Building a Resilient Financial Foundation

When people rely on a salary, their income is often subject to the ebbs and flows of the economy. Economic downturns, recessions, and company restructures can impact job security, leaving individuals vulnerable to sudden changes in income. Passive income, however, is typically derived from a variety of sources that are less directly affected by job markets and specific employment conditions.

Assets such as real estate, stocks, and diversified investments are often more resilient against economic cycles. Real estate, for example, may fluctuate in market value but continues to produce rental income. Similarly, dividend-paying stocks tend to provide income even during market fluctuations. When people create money through these assets, they build a financial foundation that is more resilient against economic volatility, offering stability even when the broader economy is uncertain.

The independence gained from passive income allows people to weather financial storms with confidence. Instead of relying solely on a paycheck, which can be fragile in the face of economic hardship, people with passive income enjoy a safety net that is better insulated from short-term economic shocks.

5. Enhanced Quality of Life: Freedom to Focus on What Matters

Perhaps one of the most profound benefits of creating money is the impact it has on quality of life. Passive income not only provides financial security; it also grants people the freedom to focus on the things that truly matter. Without the need to work constantly for a paycheck, people have more time and resources to invest in relationships, personal growth, health, and experiences.

With a steady stream of passive income, people can choose how they spend their days. They're not bound by the pressures of a job that consumes all their time and energy. Instead, they can allocate resources to pursuits that align with their values and goals. This freedom to live life on one's own terms is perhaps the ultimate form of wealth. It's a freedom that allows people to shape their lives as they see fit, guided by passion and purpose rather than financial necessity.

The quality of life that passive income enables goes beyond financial comfort—it's a lifestyle that prioritizes freedom, flexibility, and fulfillment. By creating money through assets, people unlock the ability to design their lives in ways that would be impossible within the limitations of salary-based income alone.

6. Leaving a Legacy: Creating Wealth That Lasts Beyond a Lifetime

One of the most significant aspects of creating money through assets is the ability to build wealth that endures. Passive income from investments, real estate, or businesses can continue to generate income even after one's lifetime, providing a legacy that can be passed on to future generations. This kind of wealth is not just about financial security for oneself; it's about creating a lasting impact that benefits others and contributes to a family's or community's future.

Unlike a salary, which ends when one stops working, assets can grow and provide income over multiple lifetimes. This wealth, when carefully managed and passed down, offers financial stability to descendants, funding education, healthcare, and opportunities that would otherwise be out of reach. By creating money through assets, people not only secure their own financial independence—they also leave a legacy that empowers future generations.

Building a legacy is one of the highest purposes of wealth creation. It extends the benefits of financial freedom beyond the present and into the future, ensuring that wealth serves a greater purpose than merely fulfilling immediate needs. In this way, creating money becomes an enduring contribution, providing security, stability, and opportunity for generations to come.

Conclusion: Creating Money as a Path to Financial Freedom and Empowerment

The importance of creating money lies in the transformative freedom it offers. Passive income, generated through assets, provides financial security, independence, and the ability to live life on one's terms. It frees individuals from the limitations of salary-based income, allowing them to pursue their goals, withstand economic uncertainty, and ultimately build wealth that endures beyond their lifetime.

By shifting from a mindset focused solely on earning to one that prioritizes creating money through assets, individuals can step into a world where financial independence is not just a distant dream, but a tangible reality. This journey to creating money is not just about accumulating wealth—it's about unlocking the freedom to design a life of purpose, legacy, and true financial empowerment.

CHAPTER 6

MAKING MONEY BY INVESTING CAPITAL: CASE STUDY OF THE WOOD CABINS

Real-World Application of Asset Creation

In this chapter, we delve into a case study that highlights the differences between earning a traditional salary and generating passive income through strategic investment in assets—in this instance, renting wood cabins. By examining this example, we uncover how the thoughtful application of capital can yield higher returns with significantly less active effort than salaried work.

The Setup: A Friend's Traditional Approach to Income

Imagine a friend who works as a private school tutor. They put in long hours, teaching students in exchange for a steady income. They work six hours a day, earning $15,000 a year.

This setup is common, as it's a straightforward exchange: time for money. Their income is dependable but limited by the hours they can physically work.

Your Investment: A Passive Income Stream with Wood Cabins

Contrast this with a scenario where you take a different approach. Instead of relying on a salary, you decided to invest in an asset that generates income without demanding constant work: wood cabins. After saving up the necessary capital, you purchase several cabins, each of which can be rented out for $500 per month. You rent these out for a combined monthly income of $1,500.

While your friend's income is fixed to the hours they work, your income from the cabins is not limited by your daily availability. You earn $1,500 per month without the need to actively manage or oversee the cabins constantly. This investment allows you to generate income passively, freeing you from the time constraints tied to a typical salaried job.

The Lesson: Smart Investments as the Key to Financial Growth

The case of the wood cabins highlights a powerful wealth-building strategy: *strategic investment*. When capital is thoughtfully allocated into assets—especially those like real estate that can be leased or rented—it can produce a return that exceeds the income from regular employment. Unlike salaried work, which relies on trading time for money, investing in income-generating assets like real estate allows you to leverage your resources in ways that free up your time while still building wealth.

Why Passive Income Streams Matter

Passive income is a game-changer because it allows you to generate earnings without requiring continuous, hands-on involvement. In the case of the cabins, once the initial setup was complete, income flowed in with only minor, periodic management. This setup contrasts sharply with a job in which income is directly tied to time and labor. Here, you've positioned yourself to make money from the cabins regardless of how you spend your day.

Real Estate as an Accessible Path to Wealth

Real estate investments, like renting out cabins, offer a glimpse into the potential of *making money from money*. Real estate often appreciates over time, providing a steady stream of rental income and the opportunity to sell at a profit in the future. This path may not require advanced financial expertise but rather a willingness to take the initial step toward asset ownership.

Comparing Returns: A Case for Asset Creation

When we break down the math, the contrast is striking. Your friend, working as a tutor, earns $15,000 annually. Meanwhile, the cabins yield $1,500 monthly, which translates to $18,000 annually—without active, daily work. Over time, this income disparity becomes even more pronounced, illustrating how asset ownership can outperform traditional income sources. The cabins, in this scenario, are no longer just physical structures; they are wealth-generating assets that work for you, providing income while you pursue other interests.

Building Wealth with Minimal Effort

The idea of making money by investing capital isn't about avoiding work but rather about choosing to work in ways that maximize your financial returns. Smart investing doesn't eliminate effort, but it does reduce the need for constant, active labor. By shifting the focus from working to create money directly, to creating assets that yield returns, you establish a foundation for long-term wealth.

Example 2: Investing in Vending Machines for Passive Income

Imagine another scenario: instead of investing in real estate, you decide to buy a few vending machines and place them strategically around your city in high-traffic areas like schools, office buildings, and gyms. Each machine costs a few thousand dollars initially, plus a small monthly fee to keep it stocked and maintained.

The Setup: Traditional Work vs. Vending Machine Income

In this example, consider another friend who works as a part-time barista. They enjoy their job but only earn about $10,000 a year working four hours a day, five days a week. This setup provides some financial security but is limited by how many hours they can work each week.

On the other hand, by investing in three vending machines, you aim to generate passive income. Each machine makes an average of $300 per month, which may vary slightly depending on the location and season. Altogether, you're now earning about $900 per month from the machines—or $10,800 annually—without needing to be there physically each day.

The Passive Income Advantage

Similar to the wood cabin example, your income from the vending machines is not tied to your time. Once the machines are placed and stocked, they operate independently, bringing in revenue while you focus on other pursuits. Maintenance and restocking can be outsourced, allowing you to spend only minimal time overseeing the business.

The Benefits of Strategic Capital Investment

In this scenario, your investment in vending machines acts as a mini-business that generates steady income with minimal hands-on work. You're using capital to create income-producing assets that, once established, require relatively little effort to maintain.

Comparing Returns

While your friend's barista job requires daily effort to earn $10,000 annually, your vending machines generate $10,800 annually with only occasional maintenance and restocking. Over time, the return on your investment increases as you can reinvest in additional machines or new income-producing ventures, whereas your friend's income remains capped by the hours they can work.

Lesson: The Power of Low-Maintenance Assets

This example reinforces the core lesson of strategic capital investment. Investing in assets like vending machines or real estate not only frees you from the constraints of traditional work but also opens opportunities to diversify your income streams. Each vending machine becomes a "mini-business" that generates cash flow, illustrating how investing capital in low-maintenance assets can yield significant returns without demanding a full-time commitment.

In essence, your investment in vending machines mirrors the cabin strategy but demonstrates that *asset ownership doesn't have to be limited to real estate.* By creatively seeking opportunities for passive income, you're not only building wealth but also gaining the flexibility to pursue other goals while your assets work for you.

Example 3: Warren Buffett's Teenage Venture with Weighing Machines

Warren Buffett, even as a teenager, demonstrated an understanding of capital investment and asset creation. At a young age, Buffett purchased used weighing machines, restored them, and strategically placed them in local shops. For each person who used the machine, he earned a small fee. This venture was one of his earliest demonstrations of generating income by owning and maintaining assets rather than working for a wage.

The Setup: Seeing Opportunity in Old Machines

Buffett noticed that old weighing machines could be bought cheaply, repaired with minimal effort, and then placed in stores where customers would pay a small amount to check their weight. Instead of selling the machines or charging for repairs, Buffett retained ownership and collected fees each time someone used them, creating a steady income stream.

The Lesson: Finding Value in Low-Cost, High-Return Assets

Buffett's decision to invest in used machines demonstrated his early insight into asset creation. By choosing an investment that allowed for consistent, hands-off revenue, he avoided the need for a traditional job and created a self-sustaining income source. His weighing machines worked for him, earning money each time they were used without requiring his constant presence.

Comparison to Traditional Income

Buffett's venture with weighing machines illustrates that, even with a modest initial investment, it's possible to create a scalable income stream by identifying and repurposing underutilized resources. His earnings from the machines, though small on an individual basis, accumulated over time and gave him a stable income—one that didn't require him to exchange hours for dollars.

This early experience laid the foundation for Buffett's future investments and is a perfect example of how creative capital investment can lead to sustainable income and financial independence. It shows that making money is about leveraging resources intelligently, even if they are as simple as an old weighing machine.

CHAPTER 7

THE POWER OF CORPORATIONS IN WEALTH CREATION AND TAX SAVINGS

Introduction

In the pursuit of wealth creation, one of the most powerful but often overlooked tools is the corporation. Wealthy individuals and entrepreneurs have long recognized the unique benefits that corporations provide, not only as a means to structure their ventures and investments but also as a vehicle for significant tax savings. Corporations are more than just business entities; they are financial instruments that open doors to various opportunities for growth, legal protections, and a level of financial efficiency that personal income alone cannot provide.

This chapter explores the foundational concepts behind using corporations to build wealth and how these entities offer a range of tax advantages that help amplify capital. From enabling deductibles on certain expenses to deferring tax obligations, corporations grant flexibility and scalability for those aiming to expand their wealth. This is why corporations have become a key component in the strategies of many high-net-worth individuals and financial advisors.

Whether someone is launching a new business, investing in real estate, or holding other assets, understanding the role of corporations in financial planning is essential. Wealthy individuals establish corporations to shield themselves from personal liability, optimize tax structures, and ultimately retain a greater share of their earnings. In doing so, they not only accelerate wealth accumulation but also create a robust framework for sustaining their wealth over time.

By delving into the mechanisms and advantages corporations offer, this chapter will outline how anyone, from budding entrepreneurs to seasoned investors, can leverage corporate structures to maximize wealth and minimize tax burdens.

Corporations as Tools for Financial Growth

Corporations are instrumental in the wealth-building strategies of high-net-worth individuals, providing both a structural and strategic foundation for financial growth. Wealthy individuals establish corporations to centralize and organize their assets, businesses, and investments in ways that go beyond the capabilities of personal ownership. A corporation functions as a separate legal entity, which allows individuals to detach their personal finances from business activities, thereby creating a protective shield around their personal assets and reducing personal liability. This separation is a key reason why corporations offer such unique financial advantages.

Corporations provide opportunities for structured, tax-efficient growth, allowing individuals to protect and compound their wealth over time. As opposed to managing personal finances and assets separately, consolidating various income sources and investments under a corporation simplifies the management and maximizes control. Through this approach, wealthier individuals can channel their profits, returns on investments, and additional revenue streams back into the corporation, where they can be reinvested or utilized strategically without immediate taxation on personal income.

Tax-Saving Advantages of Corporations

One of the most compelling reasons wealthy individuals use corporations is the substantial tax savings these entities offer. Corporations are subject to a different tax structure from individuals, often resulting in a lower tax rate on business income than on personal income, particularly for those in higher income brackets. Here are some specific tax-saving benefits that make corporations such an attractive choice:

1. **Expense   Deductions**
   Corporations can deduct a wide range of expenses related to business activities. This includes costs for operations, employee salaries, office supplies, travel, meals, and other expenditures associated with running the business. Wealthy individuals use these deductions to reduce taxable corporate income, thus decreasing the total amount owed in taxes. For example, if a business trip includes flights, accommodation, and meals, these costs may be deducted, ultimately lowering the company's taxable income.

2. **Income** **Splitting**

Another powerful advantage of corporations is the ability to split income among family members. This strategy, known as income splitting, allows the business owner to distribute income to family members in lower tax brackets, reducing the overall tax burden. For instance, paying a family member for a role in the corporation provides them with income while simultaneously decreasing the corporation's profits, which can yield significant tax savings.

3. **Retained** **Earnings**

Corporations can retain profits within the business rather than distributing all earnings to owners or shareholders. This option allows the business to accumulate and reinvest profits, enabling the growth of corporate assets without subjecting these funds to personal income tax immediately. This retained earnings strategy is especially valuable for business owners looking to grow their wealth without continuously incurring personal tax obligations on business profits.

4. **Tax** **Deferral**

Unlike personal income, which is taxed in the year it's earned, corporate income can often be deferred. By keeping income within the corporation, wealthy individuals can control the timing of distributions to coincide with a lower tax bracket or more favorable tax year. This flexibility allows for the strategic management of income, ensuring that tax liabilities are minimized as much as possible.

5. **Capital** **Gains** **Advantages**

When corporations invest in assets that appreciate over time, such as stocks, real estate, or other businesses, they benefit from capital gains. Capital gains are often taxed at a lower rate than regular income, allowing corporations to generate wealth through asset appreciation with reduced tax obligations. Moreover, corporations in certain jurisdictions may even qualify for tax exemptions on gains from specific types of investments, further reducing the tax burden on capital growth.

6. **Asset   Protection**
   By holding assets under a corporation, individuals gain a level of legal protection. In the event of litigation or financial setbacks, personal assets are typically shielded from corporate liabilities. Wealthy individuals use this structure to protect personal wealth, as only the assets held within the corporation are at risk in the event of a lawsuit or debt collection.

7. **Pension   and   Retirement   Contributions**
   Corporations also enable owners to make contributions to retirement funds, pensions, or other tax-advantaged savings plans. Business owners can structure contributions in ways that both minimize taxable corporate income and provide for future financial security. This flexibility not only offers long-term savings on taxes but also builds personal wealth through retirement planning within the corporation's framework.

Real-World Applications and Examples

To understand how these principles work in real life, consider a wealthy entrepreneur who owns several income-generating properties under a corporation. Instead of personally owning each property, the entrepreneur establishes a corporation that holds and manages these assets. By doing so, they gain the benefits of retained earnings, deferring tax on rental income until distributions are necessary. Any costs associated with property management, maintenance, and improvement are deducted as business expenses, reducing the taxable income within the corporation.

Furthermore, because the corporation is structured with the entrepreneur and their family members as employees or shareholders, they can split income, allowing for even greater tax efficiency. By paying family members for legitimate roles within the company, the entrepreneur reduces the corporation's overall profit while enabling family members to benefit from a steady income taxed at a lower rate.

The Corporate Mindset and Long-Term Wealth

Using corporations effectively requires a shift in perspective from viewing income as personal and immediate to viewing it as something that can be strategically grown and leveraged over time. Wealthy individuals think in terms of preserving and compounding assets, using corporations to reinvest rather than simply to distribute. This corporate mindset is essential for anyone aiming to build long-term wealth.

Corporations provide a mechanism for managing and growing wealth in ways that far surpass the limitations of personal income. With the right strategies, they allow individuals to expand their financial reach and take advantage of tax laws designed to foster business growth and economic stability. For those who embrace the corporate structure, the rewards can be significant—not only in the form of immediate tax savings but also through the compounding benefits that unfold over the years.

Saving on Taxes Through Corporations

One of the most effective strategies wealthy individuals use to grow and protect their wealth is leveraging the tax advantages of corporations. Corporations are powerful tools for minimizing tax obligations, legally allowing business owners to retain a larger portion of their earnings. By utilizing various tax-saving mechanisms, corporations can deduct expenses, reinvest profits, and strategically time income distributions—all of which contribute to a lower overall tax burden.

This section explores the key ways corporations help in saving on taxes. From deductible expenses to reinvesting profits without immediate tax penalties, corporations provide multiple avenues for reducing taxable income. Understanding these strategies is essential for any business owner or investor looking to maximize wealth by minimizing tax liabilities.

Deducting Business Expenses

One of the most immediate and tangible benefits of a corporation is the ability to deduct business expenses. Corporate expenses are subtracted from gross revenue before calculating taxable income, which directly reduces the corporation's tax liability. Common deductible expenses include:

- **Operating Costs**: Rent, utilities, office supplies, and administrative costs are all deductible, lowering the taxable income for the corporation.

- **Employee Salaries and Benefits**: Corporations can deduct salaries and benefits paid to employees, including the owner, if they are employed by the company. This allows business owners to pay themselves or family members without paying taxes on these amounts twice.

- **Travel and Entertainment**: Costs associated with business travel, client meetings, and certain entertainment expenses can be deducted. For example, meals and accommodation expenses during a business trip may qualify as deductible expenses, thus reducing taxable income.

- **Professional Services**: Fees paid to lawyers, accountants, consultants, and other professionals are deductible, which is especially helpful for those who regularly seek financial, legal, or business advice to manage their wealth.

By maximizing deductions, corporations effectively decrease their tax liabilities, leaving more funds available for reinvestment or distribution to shareholders. Wealthy individuals often structure their expenses strategically to ensure they capture all eligible deductions, thus enhancing their after-tax earnings.

Reinvesting Profits and Retained Earnings

A distinct advantage corporations offer is the ability to retain and reinvest profits within the business without immediately incurring personal income tax. This is known as "retained earnings." Instead of taking profits out of the company and paying personal income tax on them, a corporation can keep earnings within the business for growth and expansion.

For example, an entrepreneur running a corporation might decide to reinvest profits into purchasing new equipment, expanding operations, or funding research and development. All these activities can increase the corporation's value and earning potential without triggering a personal tax event.

This reinvestment of retained earnings helps the business grow and may increase the owner's wealth over time.

By keeping profits within the corporation, business owners defer personal tax obligations, a strategy that becomes especially powerful when paired with other long-term financial planning tools. Deferring income through retained earnings allows individuals to delay taxation until they are in a lower tax bracket or until they need the income, allowing for greater financial flexibility.

Tax Deferral and Strategic Distributions

Corporations provide the ability to defer taxes by controlling the timing and amount of income distributed to the owners or shareholders. For wealthy individuals, this is an essential tool for managing tax liabilities, as it allows them to choose when to take income based on tax considerations.

For instance, a corporation could retain earnings during a high-income year, avoiding personal income taxes at high rates. The business owner could then choose to distribute these earnings during a lower-income year or strategically time distributions when they have other deductions available. This approach allows the business owner to optimize tax efficiency, as they can avoid paying higher taxes on income received in a high-tax bracket year.

Capital Gains Tax Advantages

When corporations invest in assets that appreciate, such as real estate or stocks, they benefit from favorable capital gains tax treatment. Capital gains are typically taxed at a lower rate than regular income, meaning that the corporation can retain more of the profits from these investments. This is particularly advantageous for wealthy individuals, as it allows them to generate wealth through asset appreciation while minimizing the tax burden associated with these gains.

In certain cases, capital gains generated within a corporation may even qualify for exemptions or special deductions, depending on the jurisdiction and the type of assets held. This preferential tax treatment on capital gains allows individuals to benefit from asset growth within a corporation while paying less in taxes, which can significantly accelerate wealth accumulation over time.

Income Splitting

Income splitting is a tax-saving strategy that allows a corporation to distribute income among multiple shareholders, usually family members, who are in lower tax brackets. By paying family members for legitimate roles within the company, business owners can distribute profits more tax-efficiently, reducing the overall tax burden on the corporation's income.

For example, a corporation could pay a family member for their work in administration or other support roles within the company. This income would then be taxed at the family member's lower tax rate, rather than the higher rate that might apply to the corporation's owner. Income splitting not only reduces the corporation's taxable income but also provides family members with earnings at a lower tax cost, making it a highly effective strategy for wealthy individuals with family-owned businesses.

Tax-Advantaged Retirement Contributions

Corporations offer the ability to make contributions to retirement plans and pension funds on behalf of owners and employees. These contributions are often tax-deductible for the corporation, further reducing taxable income. In addition, funds contributed to retirement accounts grow tax-deferred, meaning that investment gains are not taxed until withdrawals begin during retirement, typically at a lower tax rate.

For business owners, contributing to a retirement plan through the corporation is an effective way to set aside funds for the future while reducing current tax liabilities. This strategy not only ensures long-term financial security but also leverages tax laws to protect more of the corporation's earnings from taxation.

Using Losses to Offset Income

Corporations have the unique advantage of carrying forward or back losses to offset taxable income in other years. For instance, if a corporation incurs a net loss in a given year, it can apply this loss to previous years' profits or future earnings, reducing the overall tax burden. This flexibility allows wealthy individuals to smooth out their tax obligations over time, especially during periods of business volatility.

By strategically managing losses, corporations can reduce the impact of unfavorable years and better manage cash flow and tax liabilities. This strategy is particularly beneficial for corporations with cyclical or seasonal businesses, as it allows them to level out their tax obligations across profitable and less-profitable periods.

Conclusion: Corporations as Efficient Tax Vehicles

In summary, corporations offer numerous tax-saving opportunities that allow business owners to retain more earnings while fostering financial growth. Through deductible expenses, reinvestment of profits, deferred tax strategies, income splitting, and tax-advantaged retirement contributions, corporations create a financial environment that encourages wealth accumulation with minimal tax friction.

Wealthy individuals and business owners can strategically navigate tax laws to achieve significant savings and increase the compounding power of their assets over time. By harnessing the benefits of a corporate structure, they can create a robust financial foundation that enables both growth and stability, while also aligning with their long-term financial goals. Understanding and implementing these strategies is essential for anyone looking to use corporate structures to minimize taxes and maximize wealth.

How Corporations Reduce Liability

One of the primary advantages of establishing a corporation is the protection it offers against personal liability. Corporations function as separate legal entities, distinct from their owners, which means that personal assets are generally protected from business liabilities and legal actions. This structure provides a shield for personal wealth, allowing business owners and investors to take calculated risks, pursue growth, and expand their ventures with minimized risk to their personal assets. For anyone aiming to build and sustain wealth, reducing liability is a cornerstone of financial security, and corporations play an essential role in achieving this protection.

In this section, we will examine how corporations reduce liability, how they allow business owners to grow wealth while managing risk, and why this structural advantage is crucial for those focused on building long-term financial security.

Limited Liability for Owners and Shareholders

A fundamental aspect of corporate law is limited liability, which means that the owners or shareholders of a corporation are only liable for the amount of money they have invested in the company. Unlike sole proprietorships and partnerships, where owners are personally responsible for all business debts and liabilities, corporations limit financial liability to the assets owned by the corporation itself. This ensures that, in most cases, creditors cannot pursue the personal assets of the corporation's owners, such as their homes, personal savings, or other investments, to satisfy business debts.

For example, if a corporation incurs substantial debt or faces a lawsuit, only the assets held within the corporation are at risk. This protection gives owners peace of mind, allowing them to focus on growing the business without the constant fear that a business setback or legal issue could threaten their personal financial stability.

Protection Against Legal Actions

In addition to shielding personal assets from debt obligations, corporations also provide significant protection against legal actions. By maintaining corporate status, business owners can mitigate the personal impact of lawsuits or claims arising from business operations. This is particularly beneficial in high-liability industries, such as real estate, construction, and healthcare, where lawsuits can be frequent and costly.

Because the corporation exists as a separate legal entity, it can be sued or held liable without exposing the owners to personal legal risk. In the event of litigation, any settlements, judgments, or penalties are typically limited to corporate assets rather than personal wealth. Wealthy individuals often incorporate their ventures not only to limit personal liability but also to enhance legal protections, ensuring that business operations do not compromise their personal financial security.

Safeguarding Personal Assets

For wealthy individuals, asset protection is a critical element of any financial strategy, and corporations offer a straightforward method for safeguarding personal assets. By separating business assets from personal ones, owners can confidently pursue new opportunities without risking personal resources. For example, a real estate investor might form a separate corporation to own each property, isolating the risk of one property from impacting the others or their personal wealth.

This isolation of assets helps prevent a "domino effect" where issues in one area of business spill over to affect personal finances or other investments. Even if one corporate entity faces financial or legal troubles, personal wealth and assets in other corporations remain shielded. Wealthy individuals often diversify their corporate holdings in this way, creating multiple corporations to compartmentalize risk and enhance asset protection.

Managing Debt and Credit Risks

Corporations enable owners to take on debt for business purposes without endangering personal assets. If a corporation needs to borrow money to finance expansion, purchase equipment, or invest in inventory, it can do so in its own name. If the business cannot repay the debt, creditors can generally only claim corporate assets, leaving personal wealth untouched. This structure is beneficial for entrepreneurs looking to expand without taking on personal financial risk.

Additionally, corporations often have greater access to capital, as lenders and investors recognize that corporate entities provide both a structured system for managing debt and a clear separation between business and personal finances. This separation enhances the corporation's creditworthiness and allows it to leverage debt for growth purposes more effectively than an individual might, all while minimizing the owner's personal exposure to financial risk.

Reducing Risk Through Business Insurance

Corporations can purchase insurance policies to further limit exposure to liability. By insuring against risks specific to the business's industry—such as liability for defective products, workplace injuries, or data breaches—a corporation can cover potential liabilities with insurance funds rather than corporate or personal assets.

For instance, a corporation engaged in manufacturing can carry product liability insurance, which protects against claims related to product defects, injuries, or damages caused by the company's products. Similarly, corporations can obtain property insurance, general liability insurance, and directors and officers (D&O) insurance, all of which add layers of financial protection and reduce liability exposure for the business and its owners.

Maintaining Corporate Formalities for Liability Protection

For corporations to maintain the protective benefits of limited liability, it is essential to observe corporate formalities and avoid blending personal and business finances. Corporations must conduct themselves according to established guidelines, which typically include holding regular board meetings, keeping accurate records, and maintaining separate bank accounts for personal and corporate funds. Adhering to these formalities ensures that the corporation remains distinct from its owners in the eyes of the law, safeguarding the limited liability structure.

When corporate formalities are neglected, there is a risk of "piercing the corporate veil," a legal concept that allows courts to disregard the corporation's separate entity status if it is not adequately maintained. If the corporate veil is pierced, owners may lose their liability protection, exposing their personal assets to business liabilities. Therefore, strict adherence to corporate formalities is essential for preserving the legal and financial benefits of the corporation.

Real-World Example of Liability Protection in Corporations

Consider a scenario involving an entrepreneur who owns several rental properties through a single corporation. If one of these properties faces a lawsuit—perhaps due to a tenant injury—the corporation, rather than the individual, would typically be the defendant. Because the corporation owns the property, only its assets would be at risk, while the owner's personal savings, primary residence, and other investments remain shielded from the legal action. This protection would extend even if the lawsuit resulted in a large settlement or judgment.

By holding each property in a separate corporate entity, the owner can further compartmentalize risk. In this structure, an issue with one property won't impact the others, providing an additional layer of liability protection across a diversified investment portfolio. This example illustrates how corporations enable individuals to pursue growth opportunities while managing liability exposure effectively.

Corporations as Essential Tools in Wealth-Building Strategies

For wealthy individuals and entrepreneurs, corporations are indispensable tools in the pursuit of financial security and growth. By reducing personal liability, providing legal separation, and insulating assets, corporations empower individuals to expand their ventures with minimal risk to personal wealth. This ability to separate personal and business risks is crucial for those focused on long-term wealth-building, as it encourages calculated risk-taking without jeopardizing personal financial security.

In summary, corporations provide a unique combination of protection, flexibility, and financial efficiency that makes them central to many wealth-building strategies. The ability to reduce liability is not only a legal benefit but also a financial one, as it allows individuals to concentrate on growing their businesses, investing in new opportunities, and protecting their personal assets—all while knowing that the risks are contained within a separate legal structure. For anyone serious about building and sustaining wealth, understanding and leveraging corporate liability protection is a key component of a robust financial strategy.

CHAPTER 8

THE PSYCHOLOGY OF WEALTH: DEVELOPING A WEALTH-BUILDING MINDSET

Wealth-building is not only about strategies, investments, or financial tools. It is equally, if not more, about the mindset that drives each financial decision. In this chapter, we will explore how a wealth-building mindset forms the foundation upon which all financial success is built. The psychology of wealth extends beyond mere positive thinking or affirmations; it involves deeply ingrained beliefs, habits, and attitudes that dictate how one approaches money, risk, and opportunity.

Developing a wealth-building mindset starts with examining personal beliefs around money. For many, financial security is the ultimate goal, but for those who build wealth, financial security is just the beginning. Wealthy individuals see money as a resource to create more resources—a means of achieving freedom, enabling generosity, and leaving a legacy. They adopt a long-term perspective, often prioritizing future gains over immediate rewards. This mindset requires discipline, patience, and a willingness to think differently from the crowd.

Adopting a Wealthy Mindset: Shifting from Consumer Thinking to Investor Thinking

One of the most significant shifts in the journey toward wealth-building is moving from a consumer mindset to an investor mindset. In our society, most people are conditioned to view money as a tool for consumption—a means to buy things, satisfy desires, or attain a certain lifestyle. However, wealthy individuals view money very differently. For them, every dollar is more than just spending power; it's an employee—a resource that works for them day and night to generate more wealth.

Seeing Money as an Investment Tool, Not a Spending Tool

The first step in adopting a wealthy mindset is reframing money's purpose. Where consumer thinking sees each dollar as something to be exchanged for products, services, or experiences, investor thinking sees each dollar as capital that can be grown. This shift involves viewing every dollar as an opportunity to build long-term financial security and freedom.

To wealthy individuals, each dollar invested is a step closer to greater autonomy and choice. While a consumer may focus on acquiring objects or experiences to enhance their present, an investor focuses on creating assets that will enhance their future. This requires patience and discipline, as it often means delaying immediate gratification. For instance, instead of buying the latest gadgets or an expensive car, someone with an investor mindset may choose to direct that money toward assets like stocks, real estate, or a business venture that will generate passive income over time.

Transforming Every Dollar into a Working Employee

The wealthy often talk about money as if it's a workforce under their command. This analogy underscores the concept that, rather than spending or hoarding cash, the wealthy deploy it strategically to work on their behalf. When viewed as employees, each dollar becomes part of a team dedicated to achieving financial growth and independence.

Consider each dollar you earn as a new recruit in your financial "business." A consumer might be inclined to "lay off" that dollar by spending it on something that doesn't generate a return, like entertainment or discretionary purchases. However, a person with an investor mindset would think, "How can I put this dollar to work?" In other words, they look for ways to invest that dollar where it can grow, multiplying into even more dollars. This could be through investing in assets, funding new business opportunities, or contributing to retirement accounts that accrue interest or compound returns.

From Spending to Strategic Allocation

Adopting an investor mindset involves replacing impulse-driven spending habits with a strategy of allocation. This doesn't necessarily mean giving up all luxuries but instead being mindful of where each dollar goes. Wealthy individuals are often intentional with their spending, ensuring that a significant portion of their income is allocated to investments that yield returns.

Consider how a typical consumer might use a $1,000 bonus from work. Often, this money is seen as "extra," leading to unplanned splurges or luxuries. In contrast, a wealthy person views the same $1,000 as an opportunity to build future wealth. They might invest it in stocks, use it as a down payment on a rental property, or fund a small business idea. Over time, these strategic allocations can generate dividends, rental income, or business profits, creating a steady flow of passive income that supports and even accelerates the path to wealth.

Practicing Financial Discipline and Patience

Moving from consumer thinking to investor thinking also requires a different kind of discipline and patience. The wealthy understand that real wealth is not built overnight. Investing money with the intention of letting it grow takes a long-term perspective that isn't always easy. It requires the patience to wait for compounding returns and the discipline to resist short-term spending temptations.

This mindset shift is best illustrated through the concept of compounding. By reinvesting profits rather than cashing them out immediately, individuals can see their money snowball into larger sums over time. For example, investing in a stock portfolio that yields annual returns of 8% might seem slow initially, but as returns compound, that portfolio grows exponentially. This approach necessitates the ability to resist impulsive withdrawals and to keep focused on long-term wealth generation.

Embracing Ownership and Control

Another key aspect of the wealthy mindset is an affinity for ownership and control. Consumers are often satisfied with simply participating in markets as buyers. Investors, however, seek ownership stakes—whether in stocks, real estate, businesses, or other assets—because they understand that ownership provides leverage, growth potential, and control over one's financial future.

In essence, adopting an investor mindset means choosing to be an owner, not just a consumer. Instead of paying for products or services, wealthy individuals think about how to own the assets that provide those products and services. They prioritize purchasing shares in companies over buying products from them, or owning rental properties over paying rent, because they know ownership generates income and can appreciate over time.

Shifting from Scarcity to Abundance

Finally, moving from consumer thinking to investor thinking involves embracing a mindset of abundance rather than scarcity. Many people see money as something scarce, limited to what they earn from their job. This scarcity mentality leads to holding onto money too tightly or spending it impulsively out of fear that it won't be available later.

Wealthy individuals, on the other hand, believe that money is abundant and renewable. They understand that, when invested wisely, money can grow, creating more money in the process. This abundance mentality allows them to take calculated risks and make investments with confidence, knowing that their money can yield returns.

Discipline and Patience: Long-term Wealth Requires a Mindset of Delayed Gratification

Building long-term wealth demands more than just making smart investments—it requires discipline and a patient mindset centered on delayed gratification. For many, the urge to experience the rewards of financial success immediately can be strong. But those who attain lasting wealth know that patience and delayed gratification are fundamental to allowing assets the time they need to grow and produce sustainable income.

Understanding the Value of Delayed Gratification

Delayed gratification means resisting the temptation to enjoy short-term rewards in favor of more significant gains in the future. This mindset is critical for wealth-building because most income-generating assets, like real estate, stocks, and businesses, need time to mature and yield returns. When you invest in an asset, you plant a seed that, with time, will grow and eventually bear fruit. Just as a tree doesn't grow overnight, financial success is often the result of sustained patience and a willingness to defer immediate pleasures.

In practical terms, delayed gratification involves putting off spending on non-essential items so that the money can be invested in assets that appreciate over time. For instance, instead of spending on luxury items, vacations, or frequent dining out, those focused on building wealth might channel that money into savings, investments, or business ventures. This choice allows their money to work for them, generating income and compounding over time.

Compounding Growth: The Rewards of Patience

The principle of compounding is one of the most powerful tools in wealth-building and a key reason why patience is so critical. When money is invested and allowed to grow, the returns earned on that investment begin to generate additional returns themselves. Over time, this process leads to exponential growth, turning small initial investments into substantial sums.

Consider an investment in the stock market, where a typical annual return might be around 8%. If you invested $10,000 today and left it untouched, it could grow to nearly $22,000 in ten years. With more time, say 30 years, that same $10,000 would grow to almost $100,000, simply by letting compound interest do the work. The ability to delay gratification means resisting the urge to cash out early and instead allowing investments to compound over time, ultimately building a much larger pool of wealth.

Consistent Discipline in Wealth-Building Habits

Building wealth through delayed gratification also requires consistent discipline. This discipline manifests in various ways, from making regular contributions to investment accounts to sticking to a budget that prioritizes savings over spending. A disciplined investor doesn't stray from their long-term financial goals due to short-term impulses or market fluctuations. Instead, they commit to a steady path, understanding that wealth-building is a marathon, not a sprint.

A disciplined approach also involves consistently assessing financial decisions based on their long-term value. This could mean making seemingly small but powerful choices, like brewing coffee at home instead of buying it daily, or choosing to drive an affordable car rather than purchasing a new, luxury model. These decisions might seem trivial in isolation, but over time, they free up substantial amounts of capital for investment, allowing wealth to grow steadily.

Resisting the Urge to Cash Out Prematurely

One of the hardest aspects of delayed gratification is resisting the urge to cash out when investments begin to yield returns. As wealth accumulates, it can be tempting to withdraw funds to make large purchases or upgrade one's lifestyle. However, those with a wealth-building mindset understand the importance of letting investments grow. By keeping assets invested and reinvesting any earnings, they ensure that their money continues to work for them, multiplying and creating greater financial security in the long run.

This discipline is often observed in successful investors who reinvest dividends or rental income instead of using it for personal spending. Warren Buffett, for example, famously reinvests a large portion of his earnings back into his investments, letting them grow and generate more value over time. This approach not only amplifies wealth but also compounds the potential for financial independence.

Embracing Patience During Market Fluctuations

Patience in wealth-building is especially important during periods of market volatility. When markets decline, many inexperienced investors feel compelled to sell off assets to avoid potential losses. However, those with a wealth-building mindset understand that markets are cyclical, and downturns are typically temporary. By maintaining their investments through market fluctuations, they position themselves to benefit when the market recovers, often with greater returns.

This type of patience requires emotional resilience and a steadfast commitment to long-term goals. Instead of reacting impulsively to economic downturns, disciplined investors stay focused on their long-term strategy. This focus allows them to take advantage of investment opportunities when prices are low, further fueling their wealth-building process.

Long-Term Vision Over Short-Term Gains

To truly build lasting wealth, it's crucial to adopt a long-term vision that transcends immediate rewards. The wealthiest individuals understand that their journey is not about hitting quick milestones or cashing in on short-term profits. Instead, they focus on building a robust financial foundation that will continue to support them and future generations. This long-term approach transforms wealth-building into a process that doesn't merely secure personal success but leaves a legacy.

Viewing wealth-building as a long-term endeavor often influences lifestyle choices as well. Many wealthy individuals avoid making major lifestyle changes as their wealth grows, maintaining modest habits and allowing more of their wealth to be reinvested. This perspective keeps them grounded and helps build an even stronger financial future without succumbing to the temptations of an upgraded lifestyle that doesn't contribute to their goals.

Building Wealth with Patience and Purpose

Ultimately, discipline and patience form the backbone of any effective wealth-building strategy. Without these traits, it's easy to become distracted by immediate desires or discouraged by temporary setbacks. However, those who can delay gratification and stay disciplined in their approach to investing and saving have a distinct advantage. They're able to focus on creating a future of lasting financial security, using their assets strategically to generate income over time.

By embracing delayed gratification and consistent discipline, anyone can make the shift from short-term thinking to a long-term wealth-building mindset. This mindset values the future over the present, emphasizes growth over instant rewards, and builds a foundation for sustainable wealth. With time, patience, and purpose, these qualities empower individuals not only to accumulate wealth but to cultivate a life of financial independence and freedo

Continuous Learning and Growth: Remaining a Lifelong Student of Wealth-Building

To achieve lasting wealth, adopting a mindset of continuous learning and growth is essential. The financial world is dynamic, with new investment strategies, economic trends, and technologies constantly reshaping the landscape. The most successful individuals understand that wealth-building is not a one-time effort but an ongoing journey that requires staying informed, adapting to change, and remaining open to new opportunities. Those who approach wealth-building with a commitment to lifelong learning are better equipped to navigate market shifts, capitalize on emerging trends, and refine their strategies over time.

Cultivating a Mindset of Lifelong Learning

Wealthy individuals know that to maintain their financial success, they must continue expanding their knowledge base. This mindset is rooted in the belief that there is always more to learn, whether it's about investing in new asset classes, understanding macroeconomic trends, or analyzing the financial implications of global events. By keeping an open mind, successful individuals are able to continuously refine their approach to wealth-building.

Lifelong learning often involves reading financial literature, attending seminars, listening to podcasts, or engaging in mentorship. A commitment to learning not only provides valuable knowledge but also fosters humility, as wealthy individuals recognize that the market is complex and often unpredictable. By embracing lifelong learning, they stay intellectually agile and prepared to adapt to whatever changes the financial world may bring.

Staying Informed About Emerging Opportunities

Continuous learning enables wealthy individuals to stay ahead of emerging trends and opportunities that others might overlook. For example, those who took the time to understand and invest in early-stage technology trends— such as the internet, renewable energy, or cryptocurrency— saw substantial returns as these sectors matured. By staying informed and aware of what's on the horizon, investors can position themselves strategically in new markets before they become mainstream.

Staying open to new wealth-creating opportunities doesn't necessarily mean chasing every trend but rather carefully evaluating each one with a critical eye. For instance, new investment vehicles like exchange-traded funds (ETFs), real estate crowdfunding, and sustainable investing have all gained popularity in recent years. Those who keep pace with these developments are better able to diversify their portfolios and find assets aligned with their values and goals. This approach requires a willingness to step outside of one's comfort zone and explore investment areas that may initially seem unfamiliar.

Learning from the Successes and Failures of Others

One of the most valuable aspects of continuous learning is the ability to learn from the experiences of others. Wealthy individuals frequently study successful investors, entrepreneurs, and financial leaders, gaining insights into the strategies and mindsets that have led to their success. Whether it's Warren Buffett's value-investing approach, Ray Dalio's principles for economic cycles, or lessons from real estate moguls, each success story offers valuable insights and guiding principles.

However, learning from failures is equally important. The most successful individuals don't just analyze victories; they also study setbacks, whether they are their own or others'. By understanding why certain investments or businesses fail, they gain perspective on risks and pitfalls to avoid. For example, many investors learned valuable lessons from the 2008 financial crisis, recognizing the dangers of high debt, speculative investing, and overleveraging. This insight allows them to make more informed decisions and avoid repeating costly mistakes.

Adapting to Technological Advancements in Finance

The rapid evolution of technology is reshaping the financial landscape, creating new opportunities and risks. With advancements in areas like artificial intelligence, blockchain, and fintech, wealth-building strategies have become increasingly sophisticated. Wealthy individuals understand the importance of staying informed about these changes, as new technologies can often enhance financial success or disrupt established industries.

For example, robo-advisors and automated investing platforms have opened up new avenues for wealth management, allowing investors to diversify portfolios efficiently and manage assets with minimal fees. Meanwhile, blockchain technology has created entirely new asset classes, like cryptocurrency and NFTs, which provide unique investment opportunities. By understanding and integrating relevant technologies into their strategies, successful individuals can take advantage of these innovations to maximize returns.

Expanding Knowledge Across Different Asset Classes

Another hallmark of continuous learning in wealth-building is the ability to diversify and expand knowledge across various asset classes. Many wealthy individuals achieve success by learning about different types of investments, from stocks and bonds to real estate, commodities, and alternative investments. This breadth of knowledge allows them to build diversified portfolios that can withstand market volatility.

For example, someone with experience in real estate investing might also learn about dividend stocks or private equity, creating a balanced portfolio that includes both tangible assets and equities. Diversifying in this way can mitigate risk, as different asset classes perform differently under various market conditions. Wealthy individuals who continuously seek to understand multiple investment types are better able to adapt to market changes and protect their wealth from potential downturns.

Seeking Mentorship and Collaborative Learning

The path to wealth-building is often enhanced by mentorship and collaborative learning. Successful individuals frequently seek out mentors—people with experience and expertise who can provide guidance and insights. Mentorship offers a powerful way to learn from someone else's journey, mistakes, and triumphs. Whether through formal mentorship programs, networking events, or casual meetings with seasoned investors, learning from others accelerates one's financial education.

In addition to mentorship, collaborative learning can be valuable. Many successful individuals belong to investment groups or financial networks where members share insights, strategies, and market knowledge. Being part of a community of like-minded individuals creates an environment of shared growth and accountability, where participants challenge each other, discuss ideas, and stay motivated to keep learning and improving.

Embracing Change and Innovation

A core element of continuous learning is the willingness to embrace change. Wealthy individuals understand that the financial world is constantly evolving, and strategies that worked in the past may not necessarily yield success in the future. By staying flexible and open to innovation, they can adapt their approach as markets shift, economic landscapes change, and new financial products emerge.

Embracing change also involves regularly reassessing personal goals and adjusting investment strategies accordingly. For example, someone who initially focused on high-growth stocks in their early career might shift toward income-generating assets like bonds or real estate as they approach retirement. By maintaining this adaptability, wealthy individuals ensure that their financial plans remain aligned with their goals and life circumstances.

Maintaining Curiosity and a Growth Mindset

Finally, continuous learning requires a growth mindset—a belief that skills and knowledge can always be developed and improved. The most successful people in finance possess an insatiable curiosity about the world and a desire to keep pushing their understanding of how wealth is created, preserved, and multiplied. This curiosity fuels their drive to read widely, engage in new experiences, and continuously refine their financial strategies.

A growth mindset also allows wealthy individuals to remain resilient in the face of setbacks. Rather than seeing financial losses or failed investments as a reason to give up, they view them as learning opportunities that deepen their understanding of risk and reward. This mindset enables them to recover quickly, learn from their mistakes, and keep moving forward with greater knowledge and confidence.

Conclusion

The journey to wealth is one of constant learning and growth. Those who attain and sustain wealth understand that they must remain students of finance, never ceasing to expand their knowledge and refine their strategies. Continuous learning not only keeps them informed about the latest trends and opportunities but also enables them to adapt, innovate, and make better financial decisions over time. By committing to lifelong learning, they cultivate a mindset that prioritizes growth, resilience, and adaptability—qualities that are essential for navigating the complexities of wealth-building and creating lasting financial success.

CHAPTER 9

PRACTICAL STEPS TO BEGIN MAKING MONEY FROM MONEY

As we've explored so far, building wealth is about using money as a tool rather than as a destination. It requires a shift in perspective—seeing money as a means to unlock new opportunities and to invest in assets that multiply its value. But how do you start? This chapter is dedicated to practical, actionable steps for those ready to embark on the path of creating money from money. These steps don't require immense starting capital, but they do require commitment, patience, and, above all, a disciplined approach to learning and adapting.

The wealthy aren't just lucky—they're often strategic, analytical, and methodical in building wealth, breaking down their goals into manageable actions. The aim here is to demystify some of the foundational steps so you can begin where you are, with what you have. In this chapter, we'll discuss straightforward ways to start generating returns on your money, even if you're working with limited capital. We'll also cover the importance of reinvesting profits, selecting the right types of investments based on your goals, and staying informed as markets change.

These steps will build on each other, helping you develop a strong foundation in wealth-building. The journey requires learning and adjusting along the way, but starting now, with incremental progress, puts you on the same path that countless successful individuals have traveled. Let's dive in and look at how to take your first steps toward turning your money into an engine for financial growth.

Identify and Assess Opportunities: Evaluating Potential Investments in Real Estate, Stocks, and Other Assets

To create wealth, knowing where to put your money is just as important as having the money to invest. When evaluating opportunities, the goal is to identify investments that will not only grow in value but also align with your financial goals and risk tolerance. Let's explore how to assess three major categories: real estate, stocks, and alternative assets.

1. Real Estate: Building Wealth through Property Ownership

Real estate is one of the oldest and most reliable means of wealth-building. Its appeal lies in its tangibility and the potential to generate both passive income and long-term capital appreciation. Here's how to evaluate real estate as an investment:

- **Location**: The location of a property can heavily impact its value. Areas with economic growth, employment opportunities, and good infrastructure often experience increased property values over time. Evaluate neighborhoods for growth potential, safety, amenities, and access to transportation.

- **Property Type and Purpose**: Determine whether the property will serve as a rental, a primary residence with investment potential, or a property to flip. Each purpose has its unique risks and benefits. Rental properties can generate steady passive income, while flipping offers the potential for faster but riskier returns.

- **Market Trends and Cycles**: Real estate markets fluctuate, often in cycles that impact buying and selling decisions. Research current market trends—such as buyer demand, interest rates, and housing supply—and consider the economic factors that might influence future value.

- **Financial Considerations**: Assess your budget for down payments, mortgage payments, and maintenance costs. Additionally, calculate potential rental income versus expenses to determine cash flow. A positive cash flow means the property generates more in rent than it costs to maintain, which is a promising indicator of a sound investment.

- **Risk Tolerance**: Real estate often requires significant upfront capital and carries risks, such as vacancy periods or unexpected repairs. Ensure that these potential issues align with your risk tolerance, and consider having a cash reserve for unforeseen expenses.

2. Stocks: Investing in Businesses for Long-Term Growth

Stocks represent ownership in a company, allowing investors to benefit from its growth and success. Stock investing can suit various financial goals, from short-term trading to long-term portfolio building. Here's how to evaluate stock opportunities effectively:

- **Understand the Business**: Before investing, research a company's industry, business model, competitive advantage, and growth potential. Ask yourself whether the company addresses a long-term market need and has the ability to sustain profitability.

- **Financial Health**: Analyze a company's financial statements to gauge its stability. Key indicators include revenue growth, profit margins, debt levels, and cash flow. Financial ratios like the price-to-earnings (P/E) ratio and return on equity (ROE) can also offer insights into a company's value and profitability.

- **Industry and Market Trends**: Consider broader trends in the company's industry. For example, tech stocks may benefit from advancements in digital infrastructure, while renewable energy stocks could grow with increased focus on sustainability. Understanding these trends can help you spot potential winners.

- **Risk and Volatility**: Stocks tend to be more volatile than other asset classes, so it's essential to understand your risk tolerance. Diversifying across sectors and industries can help manage risks, as does considering index funds or ETFs for exposure to a broad market range.

- **Investment Horizon**: Define whether you're investing for the long term or looking for short-term gains. Long-term investments are generally better suited for stocks, as they allow for compounding and mitigate the impact of market fluctuations over time.

3. Alternative Assets: Diversifying Beyond Traditional Investments

Alternative assets can include commodities, precious metals, collectibles, cryptocurrencies, and even private equity. These investments often provide diversification, acting as a hedge against the volatility of more traditional assets. Here's how to evaluate them:

- **Purpose and Portfolio Fit**: Assess how an alternative asset fits into your broader portfolio. Commodities like gold and silver, for example, are often used to hedge against inflation, while cryptocurrencies offer high-risk, high-reward potential. Make sure each alternative asset aligns with your financial goals.

- **Liquidity**: Many alternative assets are less liquid than stocks or real estate, meaning they may take longer to sell. If you need quick access to cash, this is an essential factor to consider. For example, artwork or collectibles can be challenging to offload on short notice.

- **Volatility and Risk**: Many alternative assets, such as cryptocurrencies, are highly volatile and can experience dramatic price swings. If you're comfortable with high risk, these assets might be an option; otherwise, consider less volatile alternatives.

- **Research and Expertise**: Alternative assets often require specialized knowledge. For example, investing in art requires an understanding of the art market, while private equity investments require insight into business fundamentals and exit strategies. Conduct thorough research or consult with experts if needed.

- **Long-Term Potential**: Some alternative assets, like vintage wine or fine art, may take decades to appreciate significantly. Ensure that any investment in this category aligns with your investment horizon.

Bringing It All Together: Creating a Balanced Portfolio

When assessing these opportunities, the goal is to build a diversified portfolio that reflects your risk tolerance and financial goals. Real estate may offer stability and passive income, stocks provide growth potential and liquidity, and alternative assets can add diversity and hedge against inflation.

Start Small, Think Big: Begin by Allocating a Portion of Your Income to Building or Acquiring Assets

Building wealth doesn't have to begin with a windfall or an extensive financial background. Many successful wealth-builders started with modest investments, gradually expanding over time. The key is to start with what you have, focusing on manageable, incremental growth. By allocating a portion of your income toward building or acquiring assets, you set the foundation for creating streams of passive income that can grow with time. This approach not only allows you to build financial security gradually but also reinforces habits that will be invaluable as you scale up.

Let's look at practical strategies to implement this "start small, think big" mindset.

1. Set a Savings Goal and Stick to It

Allocating even a small portion of your monthly income to an investment fund can yield significant results over time. Consider starting with an achievable goal, such as saving 10% to 20% of your monthly income specifically for investment purposes. Automating these contributions, where a designated amount is deposited directly into a separate savings or brokerage account, can make it easier to stick with the plan consistently.

The initial savings goal is to build enough capital to make a meaningful investment, whether it's a down payment on a rental property, a stake in stocks, or funds for other passive income sources. Remember that starting with small but regular contributions reinforces the discipline needed for long-term wealth-building.

2. Prioritize Investments with Low Entry Barriers

When just starting out, it's essential to consider investments that allow for small, regular contributions. Here are a few options:

- **Index Funds and ETFs**: These funds pool investments across a broad spectrum of companies, offering diversified exposure to the stock market with relatively low risk. Many ETFs allow you to start with small amounts and add gradually, making them ideal for beginners.

- **Dividend Stocks**: Investing in dividend-paying stocks can help build passive income over time, even with a small investment. Many companies pay dividends to shareholders quarterly, which can be reinvested for compounding growth.

- **Real Estate Investment Trusts (REITs)**: If purchasing property outright isn't feasible, REITs provide a way to invest in real estate without the high entry cost. They generate income from rental properties and distribute dividends, allowing you to gain exposure to real estate markets with limited capital.

- **Micro-Investing Apps**: Platforms like Acorns, Robinhood, and Stash allow you to invest with minimal starting capital, making it easy to get a feel for investing. These apps round up your purchases to the nearest dollar, investing the difference in diversified portfolios, which can build up over time without a large upfront commitment.

3. Reinvest Your Earnings to Grow Passive Income

The concept of compounding applies not only to savings but also to investments. Reinvesting the income or returns generated by your investments is one of the most effective ways to grow your wealth exponentially. For example:

- **Stock Dividends**: Instead of cashing out dividends, opt for a dividend reinvestment plan (DRIP). This reinvests dividends automatically, buying more shares and gradually increasing your ownership, which in turn increases your dividend payouts.

- **Rental Property Profits**: If you own a rental property or a share in a REIT, consider reinvesting the rental income to acquire additional properties or increase your stake in the fund. As your portfolio grows, so does your potential for future income.

- **Business Profits**: If you invest in a small business, consider reinvesting profits back into the business rather than withdrawing them. This reinvestment can fuel growth, expand operations, or even increase your ownership stake, resulting in higher potential returns down the road.

The reinvestment strategy transforms small initial contributions into larger, income-generating assets. Over time, reinvesting can exponentially increase your passive income, making it easier to scale and achieve significant financial growth.

4. Develop a Long-Term Plan and Adjust as You Grow

Starting small means focusing on achievable, short-term goals, but these steps should be part of a larger wealth-building plan. Consider establishing a timeline with checkpoints and milestones, such as accumulating enough for a down payment, reaching a certain investment portfolio value, or acquiring an income-producing asset. Here's how to structure your long-term plan:

- **Set Progressive Investment Goals**: Begin with smaller investments and set goals to scale them over time. For instance, if you start by investing in dividend stocks, aim to grow that portfolio to a point where it generates enough income to cover a monthly expense. From there, you can expand into larger assets like real estate or business investments.

- **Monitor and Adjust**: Review your portfolio and income streams regularly. As your wealth grows, you may want to shift toward more diversified investments or increase your contributions to high-performing assets. Flexibility is key to adjusting as the financial landscape—and your personal goals—evolve.

- **Stay Informed and Keep Learning**: Financial literacy is crucial to making well-informed decisions. Educate yourself on new investment opportunities, tax strategies, and market trends, and be open to adapting your plan as you learn. Many successful investors devote time to continuous learning, allowing them to stay ahead of the curve.

5. Harness the Power of Incremental Growth

The process of starting small doesn't mean staying small; it's about laying a stable groundwork to support larger goals. Wealth-building is often described as a marathon rather than a sprint, and small, steady steps are the key to reaching the finish line. Every small investment or reinvestment increases your earning potential, setting off a chain reaction that can lead to significant financial independence over time.

By using an incremental growth approach, you not only increase your wealth but also strengthen the habits and knowledge needed to manage it effectively. With time, patience, and reinvestment, your assets will compound and multiply, putting you in a position to achieve even your most ambitious financial aspirations.

Utilize Your Capital Wisely: Invest with a Focus on Long-Term Gains Rather than Quick Returns

One of the cornerstones of wealth-building is learning to use capital effectively, aiming for steady growth rather than chasing fast profits. Many wealthy individuals view every dollar as a potential investment, understanding that wise, long-term investments yield consistent and often more significant results than impulsive, high-risk decisions. In this section, we'll examine why it's crucial to prioritize long-term gains, the mindset shift required to do so, and how to strategically invest your capital for sustainable growth.

1. Embrace the Power of Compounding for Sustainable Growth

The principle of compounding—earning returns on your reinvested returns—drives exponential wealth growth. By investing with a long-term perspective, you allow compounding to work in your favor. Here's how to make compounding a central part of your investment strategy:

- **Reinvest Dividends and Profits**: When you receive dividends from stocks, returns from rental properties, or profits from other investments, reinvest rather than withdraw them. By doing this, you not only grow your principal but also increase the amount that earns returns, accelerating the compounding effect.

- **Avoid Panic Selling**: Market fluctuations are inevitable. Many people react to market downturns by selling investments, often at a loss. A long-term focus requires patience and an understanding that markets recover over time. Resisting the urge to panic sell allows your investments the chance to rebound and continue compounding.

- **Seek Growth-Oriented Investments**: Look for investments designed to grow steadily over time, such as stocks in established companies, real estate in appreciating markets, or index funds that track the broader market. These investments may not offer quick profits, but they provide stability and growth over the long haul.

2. Avoid Get-Rich-Quick Schemes and High-Risk Speculation

Fast gains can be alluring, but they often come with equally high risks. Speculative investments—those made without a clear understanding of the asset or market—can lead to substantial losses. Here's why caution is essential when tempted by get-rich-quick schemes:

- **Recognize the High Risk of Quick Gains**: High-reward investments often carry high risk, and without thorough analysis, they can lead to substantial losses. For example, investing in volatile cryptocurrencies or speculative stocks without understanding the market dynamics can wipe out your capital if prices fluctuate unpredictably.

- **Understand the Cost of "Fast Money"**: High-risk investments can deliver fast returns, but they can also create emotional turmoil, causing stress and potentially leading to irrational decisions. When you're investing for quick gains, you're also likely missing out on the steady growth of safer, long-term assets.

- **Stay Disciplined and Think Long Term**: Wealth-building requires discipline. Avoid impulsive investments, and instead, focus on strategies with proven, long-term results. Diversifying across assets like real estate, stocks, bonds, or other reliable vehicles will yield greater consistency and resilience in your portfolio.

3. Evaluate Each Dollar as an Investment in Your Future Wealth

A long-term perspective on capital management is about seeing each dollar as more than just money in your account. It's a piece of your future wealth—money that, if invested wisely, can grow and multiply over time. Here's how to make this perspective actionable:

- **Prioritize Value Over Cost**: Consider not just the immediate price of an investment but the value it can create over time. For example, an asset that costs more upfront but appreciates significantly over years can be a better choice than a cheaper option with limited growth potential.

- **Perform Cost-Benefit Analyses**: For every investment, ask, "What is the potential return, and how long will it take to realize it?" Weigh the costs—such as fees, maintenance, or time commitment—against expected gains. If the long-term benefits justify these costs, then the investment aligns well with a wise, future-oriented approach.

- **Set Clear Investment Goals**: Defining your goals—such as retirement savings, funding for education, or long-term financial independence—can help you allocate capital with purpose. When you know why you're investing, it becomes easier to focus on opportunities that align with these goals rather than high-risk, short-term options.

4. Diversify with a Focus on Long-Term Asset Classes

Diversification spreads risk, enhancing the stability of your investments. It also enables you to benefit from different types of growth across various markets and economic cycles. Focusing on long-term asset classes that align with your risk tolerance and financial goals is essential to achieving lasting wealth. Here are some key asset classes to consider:

- **Equities (Stocks)**: While individual stocks can be volatile, a well-diversified stock portfolio generally appreciates over time. Investing in index funds or

ETFs offers broad market exposure, reducing the risk associated with single-stock investments.

- **Real Estate**: Properties typically appreciate over time and can provide a steady stream of rental income. Real estate is often less volatile than stocks, making it a popular choice for long-term investments.

- **Bonds**: Bonds provide predictable returns and are often more stable than stocks. Although bonds typically offer lower returns, they can balance out riskier investments in your portfolio.

- **Alternative Assets**: These include assets such as commodities, precious metals, and private equity. While they may carry higher risk, they can also provide additional growth and protection against inflation when used wisely.

5. Maintain a Growth-Oriented Mindset

Utilizing capital wisely is not only about where you invest, but also how you approach the journey of wealth-building. The growth-oriented mindset is about patience, discipline, and resilience. It's understanding that wealth grows through the consistent application of sound principles rather than a one-time lucky investment. Here's how to cultivate this mindset:

- **Stay Informed**: Continuously educate yourself on financial markets, investment opportunities, and economic changes. The more informed you are, the better you can make decisions that align with a long-term vision.

- **Regularly Review and Rebalance**: As your financial situation and goals evolve, your investments may need adjustment. Regularly review your portfolio to ensure it remains balanced and continues to serve your long-term objectives.

- **Practice Delayed Gratification**: Long-term gains require delayed gratification—the willingness to forgo immediate rewards for more substantial future results. Cultivating patience allows your investments the time they need to appreciate and mature.

In Summary

Using your capital wisely means understanding that every dollar invested thoughtfully has the potential to multiply over time, building a stable financial foundation for the future. By focusing on long-term gains, avoiding quick-win temptations, diversifying across asset classes, and maintaining a growth-oriented mindset, you can transform your money into a powerful tool for lasting wealth. Wealth-building requires patience, discipline, and the wisdom to see each dollar as a seed for future prosperity—nurture it wisely, and it will grow to meet your biggest financial ambitions.

CHAPTER 10

CONCLUSION – EMBRACING FINANCIAL FREEDOM

BECOMING A MONEY MAKER, NOT A MONEY EARNER

The journey to financial freedom is not just about accumulating wealth but understanding money's true potential—as a powerful tool for creating more wealth. Moving from the mindset of a "money earner" to that of a "money maker" requires not only the right skills and strategies but a transformation in how we view money, risk, and opportunity.

10.1 Shifting Perspectives on Money

Financial freedom is often viewed as a state where one no longer worries about meeting basic needs, but it goes deeper.

True financial freedom means having choices. By stepping out of the traditional "work for money" cycle and into "make money work for you," you unlock the ability to shape your life independently of income from labor. This shift, however, begins with redefining money's purpose in your life: instead of a reward to spend, it becomes a tool to deploy strategically.

10.2 Becoming a Money Maker

The essence of becoming a money maker is understanding the creation of wealth through assets. While money earners trade time for a wage or salary, money makers look for ways to make capital work on their behalf, whether through investing, building businesses, or creating passive income streams. This requires a mindset of proactive financial planning, strategic investing, and disciplined saving, focusing on long-term gains rather than short-term indulgences.

One significant step toward becoming a money maker is adopting an investment mentality. Instead of working for wages, money makers direct their energy into growing wealth through assets like real estate, stocks, or businesses. They understand that wealth multiplies through compounding and strategic investment, not through linear labor. With every dollar earned, they ask, "How can I make this dollar generate more?"

10.3 The Power of Patience and Discipline

Patience and discipline form the foundation of wealth creation. Financial freedom doesn't happen overnight; it's a gradual process of small, consistent actions. Every wise financial decision compounds over time, leading to exponential growth. Developing patience means resisting the temptation to spend impulsively and understanding that true wealth grows with time. Discipline comes from managing one's finances responsibly, making informed choices, and staying committed to long-term goals even when immediate gratification beckons.

The path of a money maker is filled with opportunities to learn and grow. Sometimes, there will be setbacks or unexpected costs. But resilience is a crucial trait. Money makers understand that mistakes are part of the journey, using them as learning experiences to refine their strategy and strengthen their resolve.

10.4 A Roadmap for Continued Growth

Financial freedom is not an endpoint but a dynamic process of growth and adaptation. The steps outlined in this book provide a roadmap to achieving financial independence, but every individual's journey will look unique. As you move forward, remember to:

1. **Continue Educating Yourself** – Financial literacy is a lifelong pursuit. Stay informed about market trends, economic policies, and new investment opportunities. The more knowledgeable you are, the better equipped you'll be to make savvy financial choices.

2. **Reevaluate Your Goals Regularly** – As life changes, so do financial goals. Periodically reviewing your objectives ensures that your investments and strategies align with your current lifestyle and future ambitions.

3. **Diversify and Adapt** – Diversification is essential for protecting and growing wealth. By spreading investments across different assets, you reduce risk and increase the potential for returns. But also be ready to pivot and adapt to new circumstances, whether it's exploring a new industry, investing in

emerging markets, or adopting technology that can enhance your wealth-building efforts.

4. **Embrace a Mindset of Abundance** – Scarcity thinking limits potential. Money makers believe that wealth is not fixed; it is created. By focusing on value creation—both in your own life and in the lives of others—you attract opportunities and foster an environment where wealth can thrive.

10.5 Your Financial Freedom Blueprint

As you finish this book, recognize that every step toward financial freedom represents a deliberate choice to pursue independence. Whether you are just starting with modest savings or already have an established portfolio, the journey ahead requires commitment and a forward-thinking mindset.

Let this conclusion serve as both a reminder and a call to action: You are in control of your financial destiny. By adopting the principles of money making over money earning, you have the foundation needed to build wealth and secure the freedom that allows you to live life on your terms.

Building a Legacy

True wealth transcends the accumulation of money or assets. It's about creating something lasting—something that will continue to provide security, opportunity, and inspiration for future generations. Building a legacy means shifting the focus from short-term financial gains to long-term impact, crafting a foundation of wealth that grows and serves as a positive force well beyond your lifetime.

1. What Defines a Legacy?

A legacy represents more than financial success; it encompasses the values, principles, and impact that one leaves behind. In the context of wealth, a legacy serves as a vehicle for ongoing financial growth, but it also passes down knowledge, discipline, and opportunity. True wealth isn't just inherited assets—it's the mindset, skills, and understanding of financial stewardship that can empower generations to come.

Legacy-building takes time, dedication, and careful planning. It means making choices that not only benefit your immediate circumstances but also contribute to a framework that others can build upon. When done well, a legacy serves as both a financial foundation and a source of wisdom, instilling a mindset of responsibility, patience, and a vision for sustained growth.

2. The Power of Compounding and Long-Term Investments

One of the essential strategies for building a legacy is embracing the power of compounding. Wealth grows exponentially over time when properly invested, thanks to the principle of earning returns on both the principal amount and its accumulated interest. Starting early and staying committed to long-term investments allows wealth to accumulate in ways that short-term gains cannot.

For example, investing in real estate, stocks, or other income-generating assets creates a compounding effect where each year builds on the previous gains. This strategy doesn't just grow wealth—it establishes a financial pipeline that continues to generate income passively. By embracing long-term investments, you're setting up a legacy that works for future generations.

3. Creating a Framework for Generational Wealth

A true legacy requires a structured approach to wealth that includes financial literacy, clear estate planning, and a commitment to wealth stewardship. Creating a framework for generational wealth often involves:

1. **Educating the Next Generation** – Financial education should begin early, teaching children and young adults how to manage money, invest, and recognize the principles of value creation. When the next generation understands the foundations of wealth management, they're better equipped to maintain and grow the legacy.

2. **Establishing Trusts and Estate Plans** – Legacy planning involves creating structures like trusts, wills, and estate plans that legally and financially secure your assets. Trusts can ensure that wealth is distributed in ways that align with your values and goals, protecting it from mismanagement or external risks.

3. **Documenting Core Values and Principles** – Wealth management includes not just assets but the values associated with them. Leaving a record of the principles that guided your financial decisions—like discipline, delayed gratification, and long-term planning—provides a foundation for future generations to carry forward these beliefs, making wealth preservation a conscious effort.

4. Impact Beyond Finances: Philanthropy and Social Contribution

Building a legacy also means considering the broader impact of your wealth. Many individuals choose to incorporate philanthropy into their legacy, using their resources to support causes they're passionate about. Philanthropy can take many forms, from setting up charitable foundations to supporting educational scholarships or community projects. By giving back, you not only enrich the lives of others but also inspire future generations to view wealth as a means for positive change.

For some, creating a legacy includes instilling a sense of social responsibility, showing that wealth is not only to be preserved but also shared in meaningful ways. This broadens the concept of a legacy to include a positive impact on society, a goal that transcends financial metrics and influences communities for the better.

5. Preparing for a Future Beyond Your Control

True legacy building requires a level of preparation that goes beyond any immediate financial planning. It involves preparing for a time when you may no longer have control, ensuring that the assets and principles you leave behind can sustain and evolve independently. This means selecting trustworthy advisors, educating heirs, and building flexibility into your wealth structures to adapt to future circumstances.

6. The Emotional and Psychological Legacy

Beyond money, your legacy includes the emotional and psychological attitudes toward wealth. By demonstrating resilience, discipline, and a commitment to purposeful wealth management, you provide a model for future generations. Showcasing how to manage both success and setbacks prepares them to handle their inheritance with a balanced perspective.

7. Final Thoughts on Legacy Building

Building a legacy isn't about quick wins or instant gratification; it's a lifelong commitment to creating something of enduring value. A legacy serves as a testament to the life you've lived, capturing the essence of your values, achievements, and aspirations. Through thoughtful planning and intentional wealth creation, you lay a path for future generations to follow, equipping them not only with financial resources but with a mindset that honors responsibility and possibility.

.

Living on Your Terms

The ultimate goal of wealth-building is to achieve financial independence—a state where you are free to live according to your own values, dreams, and desires, unbound by the need to earn a paycheck. Living on your terms means having the financial security to make choices that align with your priorities, supported by the assets you've accumulated through disciplined and intentional investing. This chapter explores the concept of financial independence and how to structure your life to maximize the benefits of the wealth you've created.

1. Defining Financial Independence

Financial independence is often misunderstood as simply having enough money to retire or cover living expenses without working. However, true financial independence is deeper: it's about the freedom to choose how you spend your time, pursue your passions, and live your life without being constrained by financial obligations. It's the power to shape your life according to your own rules, with assets that provide stability and security regardless of economic shifts.

This level of independence requires a combination of financial planning, asset accumulation, and a mindset focused on sustaining wealth rather than merely consuming it. It involves building streams of passive income—through investments, businesses, or other assets—that cover your expenses and allow you to explore life beyond traditional work.

2. Creating Multiple Income Streams for Stability and Flexibility

To live life on your own terms, it's crucial to establish multiple income streams. Relying on a single income source, like a salary or primary investment, can leave you vulnerable to unexpected financial disruptions. By diversifying income sources, you reduce risk and gain flexibility. These streams might include:

- **Investment Income**: Dividends, interest, and capital gains from stocks, bonds, and mutual funds.

- **Real Estate Income**: Rental properties provide ongoing income while appreciating in value.

- **Business Ventures**: Businesses, whether fully automated or partially managed, can offer significant income streams and asset value.

- **Royalties or Licensing Fees**: Intellectual property like books, patents, or software can generate recurring income with minimal upkeep.

Each income source contributes to your overall financial security, enabling you to make decisions based on your goals and values rather than financial necessity.

3. Aligning Financial Independence with Personal Goals

Achieving financial independence gives you the freedom to design a lifestyle that aligns with your deepest values and aspirations. Instead of making decisions based on financial need, you can focus on what genuinely fulfills you. This might mean traveling, dedicating time to creative projects, starting a philanthropic foundation, or even spending more time with family and friends.

Living on your terms is highly personal. For some, it means retiring early and dedicating time to hobbies or passions; for others, it may involve launching businesses, traveling the world, or engaging in charitable work. The essential point is that wealth gives you the flexibility to choose and pursue what brings you joy and satisfaction, free from the limitations of traditional financial obligations.

4. The Psychological Benefits of Financial Independence

Beyond the financial perks, achieving financial independence has profound psychological benefits. Financial freedom reduces stress, enhances decision-making, and allows you to think creatively about the future. When you're not constantly worried about income or expenses, you gain mental clarity and emotional freedom, empowering you to live with purpose and intentionality.

Studies show that people who are financially independent often report higher levels of happiness and life satisfaction. They tend to feel more in control, experience less stress, and are more optimistic about the future. Living on your terms also fosters self-confidence, as you're no longer constrained by external expectations and are empowered to take bold steps that align with your vision for life.

5. Preparing for a Life of Financial Independence

Living on your terms requires careful preparation. Here are key steps to ensure that your wealth-building journey supports a life of independence:

1. **Develop a Clear Financial Plan**: Outline your income goals, budget, and investment strategy. Consider what level of passive income you need to cover your living expenses comfortably.

2. **Establish an Emergency Fund**: Life is unpredictable. Having a well-funded emergency reserve allows you to weather unexpected expenses without disrupting your financial independence.

3. **Build and Protect Your Assets**: Regularly review your investments, ensuring they align with your long-term goals. Diversify and seek professional advice to manage risk and capitalize on opportunities.

4. **Invest in Health and Relationships**: Financial independence isn't meaningful if you sacrifice well-being or connections with loved ones. Allocate time and resources to maintaining physical health and nurturing relationships.

5. **Stay Flexible and Adaptable**: Markets change, and so do personal circumstances. Flexibility allows you to adjust your financial strategy, income streams, and spending habits as needed.

6. The Joy of Living on Your Own Terms

Financial independence enables you to live a life that is genuinely yours. When financial constraints no longer dictate your choices, you have the power to define your day-to-day reality and pursue goals that resonate with your inner aspirations. Living on your terms brings joy, satisfaction, and a sense of accomplishment that enriches every area of life.

Imagine waking up each day with the freedom to choose how you spend your time, unconstrained by the pressures of a job or financial worries. This kind of autonomy opens doors to new experiences, creativity, and self-discovery. It allows you to contribute positively to the world around you, knowing that your financial foundation supports your efforts.

7. Final Thoughts on Living Life on Your Own Terms

Building a life on your terms is the culmination of disciplined wealth-building and wise financial choices. It requires patience, vision, and resilience, but the reward is a life that reflects who you truly are. By taking control of your finances, building assets, and pursuing independence, you create a life unbounded by convention, driven by passion, and filled with opportunities to explore, grow, and give back.

Living on your terms is more than just a goal—it's the ultimate expression of financial success and personal freedom. It is the reward for years of planning, discipline, and courage, granting you the ability to shape your destiny and live authentically. This journey to financial independence leads to the joy of knowing that you're free to live as you choose, empowered by the wealth you've built.

Loved the Book?
YOUR REVIEW MATTERS!

amazon

AN AMAZON KDP

Loved the review
on your book?

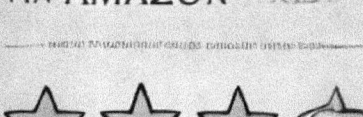

amazon.KDP

www.ingramcontent.com/pod-product-compliance
Lightning Source LLC
Chambersburg PA
CBHW071500220526

45472CB00003B/869